More Praise for *Rethinking Depression*

"This book helps us to understand ⟨...⟩ ⟨...⟩ suffering have been transformed into ⟨...⟩ psychological disorder called 'depression,' and why ⟨...⟩ transformation has left us all 'sicker and weaker' than we might otherwise be. The suggested remedy to our modern alienation, the injunction to abandon the search for happiness and to live according to our principles, stands as a challenge and an inspiration to us all. I would recommend this book to sufferers and professionals and anyone who is interested in a deeper understanding of mental health issues."

— Joanna Moncrieff, author of *The Myth of the Chemical Cure* and senior lecturer in social and community psychiatry, University College London

"The world is shrinking and the American model of mental illness is being sold globally. Soon there will be billions of 'depressed people' worldwide taking antidepressants to medicate away their unhappiness. Eric Maisel's brilliant new book explains this phenomenon with awesome clarity and simplicity and goes the next step by proposing what people can do to sidestep mental health labeling and create their own sensible program for healthy living."

— Nancy Pine, author of *Educating Young Giants*

From Reviews of Eric Maisel's Previous Books

"Eric Maisel's psychological approach sets his work apart."

— *Library Journal*

"Eric Maisel has made a career out of helping artists cope with the traumas and troubles that are the price of admission to a creative life."

Intuition magazine

"Eric Maisel's books should be required reading for anyone involved in the arts, especially students and their teachers. Maisel demystifies the process of creating art."

— *Theatre Design and Technology Journal*

"Maisel is a meticulous guide who knows the psychological landscape that artists inhabit."

— *The Writer* magazine

Praise for *Brainstorm* by Eric Maisel and Ann Maisel

"Presents a new way of thinking about how to turn brain potential into passion, energy, and genuine accomplishments."

— Camille Minichino, physicist and author of the Periodic Table Mysteries

"All too often people overlook the basics of a productive life, distracted by multitasking, marketing, and information overload. With this provocative departure from the usual lifestyle manual, the Maisels are out to break us of those tendencies."

— *Publishers Weekly*

"[*Brainstorm*] is a book that should be read by all who want to live their life in a way that is vital and leaves some kind of legacy. It's not about fame and fortune, but rather, about ensuring that this brief span that we have on Earth is one that has value — where we leave some kind of impression. There's nothing that matters more."

— *Seattle Post-Intelligencer*

RETHINKING DEPRESSION

ALSO BY ERIC MAISEL

NONFICTION

Affirmations for Artists
The Art of the Book Proposal
The Atheist's Way
Become a Creativity Coach Now!
Brainstorm
Coaching the Artist Within
Creative Recovery
The Creativity Book
Creativity for Life
Deep Writing
Everyday You
Fearless Creating
A Life in the Arts
Living the Writer's Life
Mastering Creative Anxiety
Performance Anxiety
The Power of Sleep Thinking
Sleep Thinking
Ten Zen Seconds
Toxic Criticism
20 Communication Tips at Work
20 Communication Tips for Families
The Van Gogh Blues
What Would Your Character Do?

Write Mind
A Writer's Paris
A Writer's San Francisco
A Writer's Space
Your Best Life in the Arts

FICTION

Aster Lynn
The Blackbirds of Mulhouse
The Black Narc
Dismay
The Fretful Dancer
The Kingston Papers
Murder in Berlin

JOURNALS

Artists Speak
Writers and Artists on Devotion
Writers and Artists on Love

MEDITATION DECKS

Everyday Calm
Everyday Creative
Everyday Smart

HOME STUDY COURSE

The Meaning Solution

RETHINKING DEPRESSION

HOW TO SHED
MENTAL HEALTH LABELS
AND CREATE
PERSONAL MEANING

ERIC MAISEL

New World Library
Novato, California

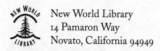

New World Library
14 Pamaron Way
Novato, California 94949

Portions of chapter 7 from *The Van Gogh Blues* by Eric Maisel. Copyright © 2002 by Eric Maisel. Reprinted by permission of Rodale Inc., Emmaus, PA 18098.
Portions of chapter 8 first appeared in *The Atheist's Way* by Eric Maisel. Copyright © 2009 by Eric Maisel. Reprinted by permission of New World Library.

The material in this book is intended for education. It is not meant to take the place of diagnosis and treatment by a qualified medical practitioner or therapist. No expressed or implied guarantee as to the effects of the use of the recommendations can be given nor liability taken.

Text design by Tracy Cunningham

Library of Congress Cataloging-in-Publication Data
Maisel, Eric, date.
  Rethinking depression : how to shed mental health labels and create personal meaning /
    Eric Maisel.
      p.   cm.
  Includes bibliographical references and index.
  ISBN 978-1-60868-020-7 (pbk. : alk. paper)
  1. Depression, Mental. 2. Mental illness. 3. Psychiatry—Philosophy. I. Title.
  RC537.M333 2012
  616.85'27—dc23

                        2011041631

First printing, February 2012
ISBN 978-1-60868-020-7
Printed in Canada on 100% postconsumer-waste recycled paper

 New World Library is a proud member of the Green Press Initiative.

10 9 8 7 6 5 4 3 2 1

For Ann,
thirty-five years into this adventure

CONTENTS

INTRODUCTION

THE REALITY OF UNHAPPINESS

I HAVE A BEAUTIFUL STORY to tell you about how you can take a stand, make personal meaning, and positively influence your moods. It is not a new story. For thousands of years existential thinkers have pressed us to get a grip on our minds and make strong choices about our relationship to life. They have advised us to seek mature happiness and make ourselves proud by boldly facing the inequities and exigencies of life. Their message: Decide to live until death wrests away your freedom.

You can lead this life of personal fulfillment, but first you must get out from under the shadow of the mental disorder model of life. Today tens of millions of people believe that they have the "mental disorder" of "depression." Maybe you are one of them. In addition, virtually everyone is convinced that, whether or not they have the disorder, it surely exists — apparently in epidemic proportions. In this book I will ask you to think through what the term *mental disorder* means, how the term is employed, and the implications of its definition. My question to you: Does the mental disorder called depression really exist?

Never — not once — am I going to say that you are not experiencing whatever it is that you may be experiencing. Never — not once — am I going to say, "Just cheer up!" Never — not

1

once — am I going to imply that nothing biological is going on. What I do hope to demonstrate is that there is something profoundly wrong with the way we name and treat certain human phenomena. When you call something a "mental disease" or a "mental disorder" you imply a great deal about its origins, its treatment, its intractability, and its locus of control. The mental health industry has its reasons for calling life's challenges "disorders," but we have few good reasons to collude with them.

I have been told that people with what we commonly call "depression" are already reluctant to come forward to receive treatment and will be even more reluctant to receive it if they become persuaded that they are "only" profoundly unhappy. Should they agree that they are only profoundly unhappy, they will presume that the solution to what ails them must be to "buck up," and they will feel too embarrassed to get help. I respect this argument and ask that readers who do feel depressed seek help. I hope that this book aids you in understanding what help to ask for from professionals and what help you should realize they can't possibly offer you.

People have also angrily informed me that the amount of pain and difficulty they're experiencing can't possibly be attributed to anything ordinary and that to imply that it can is to insult them. But the experience of pain and difficulty, no matter how severe or long lasting, is not proof of a "mental disease" or "mental disorder." Tremendous dental pain may signal with perfect accuracy the need for a root canal, but tremendous grief, which is as emotionally painful as anything under the sun, does not signal a mental disease or disorder. No amount of emotional pain is proof of these things.

Before I can paint that beautiful picture of your path to personal fulfillment, I'll spend several chapters reviewing what many critics of the mental health field have observed. In book after book they've reported the sad news that tens of millions of people have bought a bill of goods sold them by the mental health industry: that profound unhappiness is a mental disorder rather than a human challenge. I wish I could skip this discussion and move on to solutions. But because the view that a "mental disorder of depression" exists is so widespread, most people are not primed to acknowledge and make use of their innate freedom. They need their freedom back — even their freedom to feel miserable.

One of the goals of this book is to help you remove the word *depression* from your vocabulary and, as a result, from your life. If depression were an actual disease, illness, or disorder, you wouldn't be able to rid yourself of it just by removing it from your vocabulary. But since it isn't a disease, illness, or disorder, you can dispense with it right this second. What I would love is for you to say, "I can't be depressed because there is no disease of depression!" That stance would be a welcome change for millions of people. They would still have to deal with their profound and perhaps chronic and systemic unhappiness, but by dispensing with the depression label they would find themselves much better able to do so.

Family therapists like myself, who have no medical training, diagnose and treat mental disorders every day. That is what we do. I am licensed by the State of California to diagnose and treat your "mental disorder of depression," even though I have no medical training. Isn't that an inadvertent admission by the government that you have a life problem and not a medical illness or biological disorder? If your depression were *really* about your serotonin levels, your neural transmitters, or your genetic predisposition to depression, would state governments allow nonmedical personnel to diagnose and treat you?

If you actually had a medical illness or mental disorder, would state governments let psychologists, family therapists, clinical social workers, and other nonmedical mental health professionals diagnose you and treat you? Of course they wouldn't. Governments somehow know that so-called depression is a life challenge and not a disease and that sitting down and talking about it can help you a lot. The State of California is perfectly right to let me chat with you because chronic and profound unhappiness is exactly the sort of thing that I know about. That they let me do so reveals volumes about the true nature of the thing we are discussing.

You already know what it feels like to hate work or to grow so angry with your mate that you feel you are being eaten away inside. You already know what it feels like to be blindsided by despair over the fact that you must pass away in a few years. You already know what it feels like to never lose those extra forty pounds and spend your whole life unhappy about your weight. And you already know enough to make an informed decision about whether you think the mental disease or mental disorder of depression does or doesn't exist. My goal is to point you in the direction of your own knowing.

Am I alone in thinking that we've all been sold a bill of goods? Hardly. Many books have recently appeared making this same argument. Peter Conrad, for example, wrote in *The Medicalization of Society*, "'Medicalization' describes a process by which nonmedical problems become defined and treated as medical problems, usually in terms of illness and disorder. Some analysts have suggested that the growth of medical jurisdiction is 'one of the most potent transformations of the last half of the twentieth century in the West.'"

Allan Horwitz explained in *Creating Mental Illness*, "Many of the conditions encompassed by the diagnoses in the DSM [the diagnostic manual used by psychiatrists, psychologists, and psychotherapists] are neither mental disorders nor discrete disease entities; instead they reflect expectable reactions to stressful conditions, culturally patterned forms of deviant behavior, and general human unhappiness and dissatisfaction."

You may be thinking, yes, I get what you're saying; but depression *must* be something different from mere chronic or profound unhappiness. It just must be, because everybody says it is and because, well, it *just must be*. In the next several chapters we'll look more closely at the ways in which you've been trained to think that profound unhappiness is a mental disease or disorder. For now, I would just ask you to keep an open mind and begin to wonder.

PART ONE

RETHINKING DEPRESSION

CHAPTER 1

CREATING MENTAL DISORDERS

I **THINK WE CAN AGREE** that most people are made anxious by public speaking. Aren't you therefore "normal" if public speaking makes you anxious? And aren't you "abnormal" if you're able to give a speech without breaking a sweat? Since that's the case, why would we consider feeling anxious before giving a speech a symptom of a mental disorder ("generalized anxiety disorder")? Have we stepped into Wonderland, where common reactions, such as feeling anxious, are considered abnormal, and uncommon reactions, such as not feeling anxious, are considered normal?

Our anxiety in these situations is common, understandable, and normal. If it is common, understandable, and normal, how can it also be used as evidence of a mental disorder?

Just by virtue of the anxiety being unwanted.

That is the key.

Unwanted ≠ abnormal.

As soon as you employ the interesting linguistic tactic of calling every unwanted aspect of life abnormal, you are on the road to pathologizing everyday life. When you make every unwanted experience a piece of pathology, it becomes possible to knit together disorders that have the look but not the reality of medical illness. This is what has happened in our "medicalize everything" culture.

Mel Schwartz wrote in his blog for *Psychology Today*: "I would offer that what would otherwise be a normal experience of the ups and downs of being human are now viewed through the prism of dysfunction. Every challenge and travail has a diagnostic label affixed to it and we become a nation of victims — both to the malaise and [to] the pathologizing of what it means to be human."

It is a grave mistake to make every unwanted aspect of life the symptom of a mental disorder.

A heart attack may come with symptoms such as chest tightness and shortness of breath. These symptoms occur because an artery is blocked, a valve is failing, and so on. In the case of a heart attack, there is a genuine relationship between an organic malfunction and the symptoms of that malfunctioning. Unhappiness too may come with certain "symptoms," such as sleeping a lot and eating a lot. But these symptoms are not evidence of organic malfunctioning. They are what come with unhappiness.

For thousands of years human beings have made the sensible distinction between feeling sad for certain reasons (say, because they were jobless and homeless) and feeling sad for "no reason," a state traditionally called melancholia. Some people got sad occasionally, and some were chronically melancholic. Today both varieties of unhappiness, the occasional and the chronic, have been gobbled up by the mental health industry and turned into disorders.

With the rise of four powerful constituencies — the pharmaceutical industry, the psychotherapy industry, the social work industry, and the pastoral industry — and their handmaidens — advertising, the media, and the political establishment — it has become increasingly difficult for people to consider that unhappiness might be a normal reaction to unpleasant facts and circumstances. Cultural forces have transformed almost all sadness into the mental disorder of depression.

In fact, the word *depression* has virtually replaced *unhappiness* in our internal vocabularies. We feel sad but we call ourselves depressed. Having unconsciously made this linguistic switch, when we look for help we naturally turn to a "depression expert." We look to a pill, a therapist, a social worker, or a pastoral counselor — even if we're sad because we're having trouble paying the bills, because our career is not taking off, or because our relationship is on the skids.

That is, even if our sadness is rooted in our circumstances, social forces cause us to name that sadness "depression" and to look for "help with our depression." We are seduced by the medical model, in which psychiatrists dispense pills and psychotherapists dispense talk. It is very hard for the average person, who suffers and feels pain because she is a human being but who has been trained to call her unhappiness depression, to see through this manipulation.

Tens of millions of people are tricked into renaming their unhappiness depression. Charles Barber elaborated in *Comfortably Numb*: "In 2002, *16 percent* of the citizens of Winterset [Iowa] were taking antidepressants....What is compelling one in six of these generally prosperous and stable citizens to go to their doctor, get a prescription, and go to the...pharmacy? And Winterset is by no means alone...for Ames it is 17.5 percent; for Grinnell, 16 percent; Des Moines, 16 percent; Cedar Rapids, 16 percent; and Anamosa, Red Oak, and Perry, 15 percent."

Isn't that something? Not the fact that so many people feel unhappy — the number of people who are unhappy is huge. What is quite astounding is that folks in the heartland, where stoicism and common sense are legendary, should have swallowed whole hog the idea that unhappiness is a medical condition.

The first linguistic ploy is to substitute the word *abnormal* for *unwanted*. Next, since it is almost certain that profound unhappiness will make it harder for you to get your work done and deal with your ordinary responsibilities, one way to ensure that your unhappiness will be labeled "depression" is to name as a significant diagnostic criterion an "impairment of function." Maybe you're unhappy with your unsatisfying job and you start skipping work. That is certainly not a symptom of a mental disorder unless we make it one — which we can do by calling it "impairment of function."

Let's say that you're a mystery writer. You've written three mysteries and managed to sell them. But they haven't sold well enough to justify your publisher's buying a fourth mystery from you. Your literary agent is certain that no other publisher will buy that fourth mystery, either. You get that news right in the middle of writing mystery number four. What happens? You grow seriously unhappy and you stop writing your fourth novel. Why bother? The thought passes through your mind: Why bother to live? Suddenly you have no chance of ever escaping your day job. You somehow manage to go to your day job, but you find yourself working listlessly and carelessly. Nothing amuses you. Nothing interests you. You begin to chain-eat Twinkies.

In this contemporary culture of ours, you are almost certain to call yourself depressed. The instant you do so, you reduce your chances of effectively handling your painful situation. Having called yourself depressed, you'll probably take yourself to a mental health provider to whom you'll explain your situation. You'll say, reasonably enough, that you're sleeping too much, eating too many Twinkies, not writing your novel, and performing carelessly at your day job. The first two, by virtue of being unwanted, become "symptoms of a mental disorder"; the second two become evidence of "impairment in functioning." You are diagnosed with depression — which, of course, is exactly what you expected to hear. Any other outcome would have been very surprising!

The following transaction occurred: You visited a mental health professional because you were feeling unhappy and because you had already affixed the label "depression" to your state. Having affixed that label, you naturally went in search of someone trained to diagnose and treat depression. What you reported were exactly the sorts of things contrived by the mental health industry to prove that you have a mental disorder. You came in "depressed" and you received the diagnostic label "depression." Transaction completed.

That there are many things going on in your life that you wish would change or go away does not make them abnormalities. They may even "impair your functioning," but to use that phrase is to medicalize your situation. These linguistic ploys, which are now fully embraced by millions of Americans and growing millions worldwide, have transformed the human landscape, making countless people sicker and weaker than they otherwise might be.

Creating Mental Disorders

When you define something with a series of *or*s rather than a series of *and*s, you do a poorer job of distinguishing among things. If you define a table as an object with a top *and* four legs, you exclude cattle. But if you define a table as an object with a top *or* four legs, you include them. Has the thing got four legs? It's in! If you intend to include a lot of things, perhaps because that makes you more money, it makes sense that you would define those things with a lot of *or*s.

That is exactly how mental disorders are defined, with a lot of *ors*. The American Psychiatric Association defines *mental disorder* as "a clinically significant behavioral *or* psychological syndrome *or* pattern that occurs in an individual and that is associated with present distress *or* disability *or* with a significantly increased risk of suffering death, pain, disability, *or* an important loss of freedom."

This definition is specious. Critics of the mental health industry have pointed out time and again that virtually anything unpleasant meets these pointedly empty criteria. If I run too many marathons and hurt my knees, I've met the criteria for a mental disorder. (I have a "clinically significant behavioral syndrome with present distress.") If I feel elated and I treat myself to a climb up a steep mountain, I've met the criteria for a mental disorder. (I have a "clinically significant psychological syndrome with a significantly increased risk of suffering death, pain, and disability.")

You may think that in presenting these absurd examples I'm not keeping to the spirit of the definition. In fact, that is exactly the spirit of the definition, to create such a large tent that virtually anything can qualify — your son's restlessness in math class, your worry about your dwindling retirement account, your daughter's unhappiness with her college choice, your sister's trips to the casino, your brother's boredom on the weekends. Countless critics of the mental health industry have pointed out that *mental disorder* is a term used as a professional opportunity and not as a marker of a genuine medical condition.

The first step in creating mental disorders out of ordinary human experiences is to define those ordinary experiences as pathological by using phrases such as "clinically significant behavioral or psychological syndrome." The second step is to refuse to say what causes the disorder or, alternatively, to assert that just about anything might cause it. If you say that it takes sawing and joining and so forth to create a table, then you've excluded cattle from the mix of things called tables. But if you include any four-legged thing *and* you refuse to distinguish among causes (say, between natural selection and carpentry), your cattle can't be excluded. If you say that anything with four legs created any which way is a table, a cow is a table.

If you are in the business of creating mental disorders, it is very important to throw up your hands in a kind of ecumenical fervor of allowing and make sure not to say what is causing the mental disorder you've created. The mental health industry does this by saying that depression may be caused by any number of things — psychological things, biological things, social things, spiritual things, the weather, hormones, motherhood, genes, childhood, anything. This makes some kind of sense because if what they are talking about is human unhappiness — and it is — then naturally that unhappiness might be caused by anything that makes human beings unhappy. But it makes no sense whatsoever as scientific explanation. Imagine that your physician looked at a tumor growing on your arm, shrugged, and said, "Could be caused by anything" — and took zero interest in ascertaining what *was* causing it.

This leads to our next point: when creating a disorder, make sure that there are no real tests to employ to determine what is causing your depression. Your physician, having looked at your tumor, would run tests because she *is* interested and because she *does* believe that you have a genuine medical condition. Your mental health provider won't run any tests. What *could* he be testing for, if it is human unhappiness? Does he dare announce that such a test is intended to distinguish between a mental disorder and human unhappiness? Wouldn't that put it into your head that maybe you are not ill but sad?

First he defines *disorder* broadly. Then he says that almost anything might cause it. Then he avoids testing for it. Fourth, he makes very muddy the idea of cause and effect. The truth of the matter may be that your mood has caused changes in your brain chemistry; he looks at those changes and cries, "See, depression must be biological!" That is, he acts as if changes in brain chemistry caused the unhappiness — even though what actually happened was the exact opposite. He knows that very few people will pay enough attention to see through his gambit, and even if they do, their cry of outrage will fall on the deaf ears of a society not trained to think very deeply about cause and effect.

In "The Myth of Biological Depression," Lawrence Stevens discussed the relationship between cause and effect:

> Even if it was shown that there is some biological change or abnormality "associated" with depression, the question would remain whether this is a cause or an effect of the "depression." At least one brain-scan study (using positron emission tomography or PET scans) found that simply asking normal people to imagine or recall a situation that would make them feel very sad resulted in significant changes in blood flow in the brain. Other research will probably confirm it is emotions that cause biological changes in the brain rather than biological changes in the brain causing emotions.

Define the disorder broadly. Say that anything might cause it. Provide no tests. Mislead about cause and effect. Now comes the clincher: create a laundry list of symptoms that anyone who can read can use to diagnose the disorder. This is a crucial step because without this laundry list in hand the mental health provider would have no way to turn a new client's self-report of unhappiness into the mental disorder of depression. This checklist, created by industry professionals sitting around a table, is gold.

In a moment we'll create a mental disorder of our own — it's such a simple task it won't take us more than a minute or two.

In *Before Prozac*, Edward Shorter wrote: "Many of the diagnoses of mood disorder today really don't make a lot of sense.... Medicine is supposed to make progress, to go forward in scientific terms so that each successive generation knows more and does better than previous generations. This hasn't occurred by and large in psychiatry, at least not in the diagnosis and treatment of depression and anxiety, where knowledge has probably been subtracted rather than added."

Knowledge has been subtracted for the sake of a profit. The game is very easy to play. If we were in a position of power and influence within the mental health industry, we would have absolutely no trouble creating innumerable mental disorders and foisting them on an unsuspecting — and all too willing — public. Let's see how this process works by creating our very own mental disorder.

Creating Our Own Mental Disorder

First, let's choose some human experience that most people find unpleasant. How about boredom? Most people find boredom unpleasant. So let's get started and substitute the word *pathological* for *unpleasant*. Doesn't that simple switch start to make it feel like a disease already? Pathological boredom!

The next step is to name our disease. How about "interest deficit disorder" or "motivation deficit disorder"? Better yet, let's find a medical-sounding word from Latin to substitute for boredom. *Movere* is Latin for "motivation." How about "dysmoveria"? By naming our disease, we have practically created it. When you open a door to a new mental disorder, millions of people will rush headlong right through it, as if they'd been waiting their whole lives for just this opportunity. Suddenly they aren't sad or anxious or bored — they're afflicted with something.

We have our disease named: dysmoveria. It sounds a little strange now, but it won't when millions of people start using it and chatting about their disorder. "I'm taking Moveritol for my dysmoveria, and it's working wonders!"

Next we need a symptom picture. What does it look and feel like when you're bored? Well, a bored person would probably experience some or all of the following:

1. a lack of interest in usual pursuits
2. apathy
3. pessimism
4. feelings of "going through the motions"
5. difficulty concentrating on ordinary tasks
6. a lack of energy
7. chronic fatigue
8. sleeping too much or too little

How many of these symptoms must be present in order for us to diagnose the mental disorder of dysmoveria? Since obviously, if we have a vested interest in creating mental disorders, we want as many people as possible to fit the diagnostic criteria so that we can create plenty of patients and plenty of purchasers of Moveritol, let's make sure that only a few symptoms are needed in order to qualify — let's say, five. Let's continue pulling numbers out of thin air and say that these five symptoms must have been present for at least two weeks. Five symptoms, two weeks — sounds good.

Let's also make this negotiable. If only four symptoms are present and if they've only been present for twelve days, we're not going to quibble. Heck, if the "primary" symptom is present

— feelings of boredom — that's really enough! We'll call that looseness "professional discretion."

Officially you will need to display five symptoms and have displayed them for two weeks. We offer no rationale for these numbers, since no rationale is needed when creating a new mental disorder. Nor could any rationale conceivably be provided. Unofficially, all you need to do is announce that you're bored — that's all we really need to hear!

Next, if we were doing this "for real," we would gather a panel of clinicians — some psychiatrists, psychologists, family therapists, and clinical social workers — and we'd ask them, "Do your clients or patients ever report this symptom picture?" "Yes!" they'd cry in unison. "We see this all the time!" "Great!" we'd reply. "We have ourselves a genuine disorder!"

Next we'd work on "differential diagnosis criteria," that is, on distinguishing dysmoveria from, say, clinical depression, which it quite resembles in its symptom picture. How would we know which was which? Naturally enough, we would know according to the self-reports of patients. The primary differential diagnostic criterion would be that if you reported feeling sad we'd go with depression, and if you reported feeling bored we'd go with dysmoveria. Simple enough!

Next, how shall we treat dysmoveria? Well, with some combination of treatments, thus allowing everyone with a clinical practice to have patients. Whatever your license says you are allowed to do, we will say that works. Clinicians who can't prescribe medication, such as psychologists, family therapists, and clinical social workers, will be permitted to "talk it away." Clinicians who can prescribe medication, such as psychiatrists, will be permitted to prescribe. We need not provide any rationale as to why a mental disorder should be treatable just by talking about it. Talking is a completely customary way to treat mental disorders and needs no rationale.

Of course, we'd get drug researchers right on the job creating a drug that can reduce or eliminate the symptoms of dysmoveria. This will be much simpler than it sounds, since there is no actual underlying disease to be treated. If you had a malignant tumor, you'd need to treat the tumor and not just the symptoms of its presence. Here we are just treating symptoms, since there is nothing present underneath except boredom. So our drug research can be up and running instantly, since our goal is the relatively simple one of eliminating or masking certain symptoms.

An additional option, if we happen to have a few neuroscientists among our friends, would be to have them do a little brain scanning. And guess what? They would discover that a brain looks different when you have dysmoveria! Wow. When you're bored fewer parts of your brain light up than when you're excited. This kind of observation thrills people and sounds very scientific. It is completely meaningless in and of itself — of course your brain will light up in different ways depending on whether you're watching the shopping channel or doing calculus — but people take this to mean something. This is muddy cause and effect in action and as such quite a useful add-on!

Naturally, while in the process of creating mental disorders, it helps to be in a position of authority. Being a psychiatrist or having some association with a drug company wouldn't hurt. But, really, anyone can pull off the feat. Just write a book that makes the case for your new mental disorder, hire a publicist, and let's see how long it takes before patients line up! Wouldn't millions of people suddenly discover that they were suffering from "email distraction disorder" or "postretirement dysthymia" as soon as they heard about it? You bet they would!

If we follow the simple steps I've just outlined, we can turn any unwanted human experience into a mental disorder. Try it yourself with envy (invidia), rage (furorism), loneliness (infrequentia), and doubt (dubitarism). Sleeping more than usual?

Going through the motions? Not interested in what's going on around you? Apathetic? Bored? Those symptoms perfectly describe a teenager on a two-week summer vacation with her parents! But now we have a better name for it: dysmoveria. Isn't it nice that soon there will be a drug to give your daughter so that she will be more pleasant and pliable when she accompanies you on your annual trip to Nebraska?

I think you recognize the basic ruse by now. All you need to do is give an unwanted experience a medical-sounding name and describe its "symptom picture," a fancy phrase that just means what it looks like, and you've created a disorder. This unwanted, troubling experience is surely real, but calling it a mental disorder is just a profitable naming game.

Symptom Pictures

Let's talk more about the pitfalls of these symptom pictures. If a mental disorder were something like an actual illness, disease, or disorder, both you and the person treating you would want more than a symptom picture — you would want an explanation.

That symptom pictures alone are used to "diagnose mental disorders" should cause you to jump out of your chair and exclaim, "Wow, that *is* alarming!" A symptom picture is not an explanation. Your hands might be rough because you have a skin problem or because you lay bricks. Dabbing on an ointment may alleviate the symptom of roughness, whether it is caused by an ailment or by your job, but if the roughness is caused by an ailment that needs further treatment, the opportunity to recognize the ailment has been missed.

The same is true in the diagnosing and treating of so-called mental disorders. The medication you receive may alleviate some, many, or all of your symptoms, such that you are able to report that you "feel better." But if profound unhappiness and not a biological disorder has caused these symptoms, what do you suppose are the chances that you are really "cured"?

Zero.

Let's say you find yourself sitting inert for hours at a time in front of the television, eating several large bags of potato chips each day, hardly speaking to the people around you, refusing to clean your apartment, and barely dragging yourself to work. A psychiatrist looking at that symptom picture would very likely say that you're depressed and that you ought to go on an antidepressant right away.

What if what is actually going on is that you received some scathing criticism at work that sent you reeling and your sense of yourself plummeting and that you haven't yet recovered from that blow? The symptom picture without an explanation only got you drugs. The real explanation makes sense of your unhappiness and alerts you to what you need to do to actually recover: change your job, build your self-confidence, and so on.

When you rely on symptom pictures rather than explanations to diagnose human challenges, and when you create treatments intended to reduce or eliminate the symptoms of living rather than addressing the human issues involved, it is not too far-fetched to imagine a time when the clerk at your local big-box store will be empowered to scan a laundry list of symptoms, check them off, and send you to the back of the store where a doctor will dispense the antidepressant of the month. This exchange might look like the following — except that in reality it would not prove half this amusing.

You've been feeling unhappy for several weeks and decide to visit your local big-box store for help. The friendly clerk at the Depression Counter looks up and greets you cheerfully.

"Good morning, sir! How can I help you?"

"I've been feeling quite blue —"

"Absolutely! How long have you been depressed?"

"Oh, maybe for three weeks...though in another sense —"

"Not to worry! You only need to have been depressed for two weeks to qualify for our award-winning treatment program! But if you don't mind, I have a few questions for you."

"Of course."

"First, what sort of depression is it?"

"Excuse me?"

"Well, wouldn't it be nice to know what sort of depression you've got? Not that that's crucial, mind you — but wouldn't it be nice to know?"

"Gee, I suppose so — but I haven't a clue. I'm not even sure what you mean."

"Well, is your depression biological? Psychological? Social? Spiritual? Existential? Hereditary? Hormonal? Chronic? Temporary? Exogenous? Endogenous? Neurotic? Psychotic? Circumstantial? Attitudinal? A cognitive problem? Work related? Love related? About your apartment having mice? Because a cloud passed across the sun? See what I mean?"

"Gee! I surely don't know. I'm just...depressed."

"Yes, that's what our customers always say!" she exclaims, smiling brightly. "But of course that isn't very helpful."

"No, I suppose it isn't. As a matter of fact, I don't have a lot of energy to even think about this."

"That's awfully convenient!" she chides you, wagging a finger. "You're blue so you don't feel up to telling me why you're blue. Tsk-tsk!"

"Well, I'm tired. Does that help?"

"Not really. Fatigue is a common symptom of depression, but we already know that you're depressed. I've got all the symptoms right here" — she thumps a thick book with the title *Diagnostic and Statistical Manual of Mental Disorders* — "and no doubt you've got the requisite number of symptoms. But your symptoms don't help me know what depression you have."

"They don't? I thought that's exactly what symptoms *did* tell you. What's causing what a person's got, I mean."

"Well, yes, for real illnesses — oh, excuse me, that slipped out, of course you have a real illness — but for mental disorders — sorry, that's what we call your depression — well, no, symptoms don't tell us what's going on inside. They just help us give the thing a name — but you named the thing already!" she exclaims with a big smile. "You've got depression! So, no, naming your symptoms won't help me a bit."

"Gee — well, I have trouble sleeping. Does that help?"

"No! That's just another symptom! Aren't you following me? Plus, that could be a symptom of anything. Maybe you stupidly bought a house next door to the elevated subway...sorry, I was thinking of someone else."

"I've lost some weight," you offer speculatively.

"Maybe that's cancer."

"What?" you exclaim.

"Sorry. But if you just keep giving me common symptoms of depression, what am I supposed to do? Next you'll tell me that you don't find your usual interests interesting."

"Yes! That's exactly right."

"And that you're sad."

"That's right!"

"Well, boo-hoo. Oh, sorry. I should have gone on break an hour ago. This place is so depressing! — oops, I mean, well, where were we?"

"You were describing me perfectly but also telling me that even with that perfect description you don't know what depression I have. So I was thinking, maybe you have a checklist, like if it's a biological depression it looks like this and if it's a psychological depression it looks like that? That would help."

"Indeed it would. Don't have it."

"Oh."

"Nope. So you'll have to tell me. We call it 'self-reporting.' Cool, huh?"

"Well —"

"Excuse me!" She reaches across the counter and touches you on the arm. "I've just been joshing you. I don't really need to know what sort of depression you have. This week we have a special on Kumquativir! It's a new, improved antidepressant, and I am absolutely going to recommend it to you. Of course, you'll need a doctor's prescription, but not to worry — we have a doctor in the back room. Just go back there and name your symptoms, and he'll write you a prescription for Kumquativir. Now, it may make you constipated and irritable — and fifteen other things, it's all here in this pamphlet — but it is a super-cool new antidepressant, and you just *have* to try it. And we have it in cherry or strawberry."

"But you were making some sense — about needing to know what depression I have in order to get the treatment right — I mean, that did sound sensible..."

"Yes. But here's something I was taught at big-box depression school. If you call depression a bio-psycho-social thing, you've pretty much covered all the bases! Neat, huh?"

"But all those questions —"

"I was just pulling your leg."

"No, they were making some sense."

She lowers her voice confidentially. "Oh, people like that sort of thing. If we ask enough questions and take down your answers, it makes it seem as if we must be looking for something. But we aren't really looking for anything! We know from the beginning that we'll be giving you a drug, just as soon as you say the magic words!"

"What were those?"

"That you're depressed! That was plenty."

"You're joking."

"We don't joke at the Depression Counter," she says solemnly. But she can't keep from smiling. "Well, yes, we do sometimes joke, but it's really frowned on. You know, when I worked at the supermarket I was supposed to smile all the time, and here I'm supposed to be serious all the time. Go figure."

"So — it's Kumquativir for me?"

"Yes! This month it's Kumquativir!"

This tongue-in-cheek scenario will never come true because the mental health industry would fight it tooth and nail. Can you see therapists giving up their power to diagnose to shop clerks? But the fact remains that when mental health providers transform unwanted human experiences into so-called mental disorders that they diagnose in accordance with a laundry list of symptoms, they leave themselves open to ridicule.

CHAPTER 2

WHAT DO "TREATMENTS" REALLY DO?

YOU MAY BE THINKING, "Well, psychiatrists, psychologists, family therapists, and other mental health professionals surely know what to *do* with these symptom pictures. Maybe it isn't an exact science but more like an art, where, through practice, these professionals begin to discern the difference between a mental disorder and a life challenge. So, even though the system is flawed, practitioners *do* know important things about mental disorders."

You would be wrong.

An elegant experiment performed by psychologist Maurice Temerlin and published in the *Journal of Nervous and Mental Disease* makes this abundantly clear. Temerlin had an actor memorize a script that was designed to portray a mentally healthy individual (let's call him Harry). Harry was happy, effective at work, self-confident, warm, gracious, happily married, and insightful — as mentally healthy as a person can be. Temerlin interviewed Harry and taped the interview. He then played the interview for various groups of mental health professionals, informing them that Harry was a prospective patient and that they were listening to an "intake interview."

Temerlin set up three basic scenarios. In the first, a group of mental health professionals were played the tape and asked to rate Harry's mental health. In the second a well-known mental health professional informed the gathered professionals that they were about to listen to an interview with "a very rare person, a perfectly healthy man." In the third, a well-known mental health professional told the gathered professionals that they were about to listen to an interview with a man who "appears neurotic but is really psychotic." They were told not to base their rating on anything but the interview itself — that is, they were explicitly told not to use the information provided by the "prestige associate."

The results? In the first scenario, in which mental health professionals had no information about Harry other than the interview, not a single graduate student, psychologist, or psychiatrist found the subject to be psychotic (though more than 40 percent did find him either neurotic or character disordered!). In the second, in which the mental health professionals were told that Harry was "a very rare person, a perfectly healthy man," 100 percent found him to be mentally healthy. In the third, in which the mental health professionals were told that the subject "appeared neurotic but was really psychotic," almost every graduate student, clinical psychologist, and psychiatrist rated him as either psychotic or neurotic. The psychiatrists were the worst in this regard: 60 percent rated him psychotic, and 40 percent rated him neurotic.

Having listened to an interview with a healthy man and been told to confine their ratings to the evidence of the interview, 100 percent of the psychiatrists judged him disordered.

Many other experiments have confirmed that mental health professionals, when confronted by a patient or prospective patient, do not diagnose actual disorders but rather express unfounded opinions that match their training and that serve their pocketbooks. An excellent experiment run by Ellen Langer of Harvard and Robert Abelson of Yale and published in the

Journal of Consulting and Clinical Psychology further illustrates this point. The experimenters wanted to gauge what therapists would say about a subject who for one set of therapists was called a "job applicant" and who for a second set of therapists was called a "patient." Would the latter label bias their opinions?

Did it ever!

Those therapists who thought that the subject was a job applicant used words such as *candid, upstanding, innovative,* and *ingenious* to describe him. Those who thought that the subject was a patient used words and phrases such as *tight, defensive, frightened of his own aggressive impulses, conflicted over homosexuality,* and *passive-dependent type.* The experimenters concluded, "Once an individual enters a therapist's office for consultation, he has labeled himself 'patient'...The therapist's negative expectations in turn may affect the patient's own view of the situation, thereby possibly locking the interaction into a self-fulfilling gloomy prophecy."

May, indeed!

If all it takes to convince mental health service providers that a fundamentally sane person is either psychotic or neurotic is the say-so of another provider, and if all it takes to turn a person's ordinary behaviors into symptoms of pathology is to label him a patient, our eyes should be opened to a fundamental truth about diagnostic labels. The system is designed to turn ordinary human experience into categories of disorder, trapping in any real disorders with the concocted ones. This bad science couples intellectual shoddiness with venality to produce tens of millions of "patients" annually.

Robert Whitaker has more to say about this in *Mad in America*:

A dark truth became visible in American medicine in the 1990s. Bias by design and the spinning of results —

hallmarks of fraudulent science — had moved front and center into the testing of commercial drugs....When the [*New England Journal of Medicine*] tried to identify an academic psychiatrist who could write an honest review of antidepressant drugs, it found "very few who did not have financial ties to drug companies." One author of an article on antidepressant drugs had taken money from drug companies on so many occasions...that to disclose all of them "would have taken up more space than the article."

It is not that hard to explain this system-wide conspiracy to turn unwanted experiences into mental disorders. That you can make money doing it explains a lot. That you gain prestige and ego gratification by being a person who can "diagnose and treat" your fellow human beings is surely part of it. And a combination of incuriosity and intellectual shoddiness may be just as pertinent. When I sat in my psychology and counseling classes and listened to my professors' lectures, I asked many questions because what I was hearing did not make sense to me. But no one else did. My fellow students seemed to have no investment in comprehending.

When a professor said, "When you see these eight symptoms, you call it this disorder," no one (except me, until I got tired of inquiring) asked, "Why?" No one asked, "What is the relationship between diagnosing and treating?" Did that relationship seem self-evident to my fellow students? If I say to you, "When you have a depressed client, feel free to use medication, gestalt therapy, cognitive therapy, Jungian therapy, Freudian therapy, or anything you like, it's all the same," does that make sense to you? Yet that was what we were taught: diagnose according to the diagnostic manual, and then treat using your favorite treatment method.

How was Jungian therapy supposed to work on a biological disorder? How was medication supposed to work on arrested development? How was a combination of medication and object-relations therapy supposed to help a person with a depressing life? For whatever reasons — professional self-interest, ego gratification, prestige needs, distaste for rocking the boat, incuriosity, intellectual shoddiness, or some combination of these and more — no one posed these questions.

It should not surprise you that a few years after becoming a licensed therapist I switched from doing therapy to coaching. When the coaches I train ask, "What's the difference between coaching and therapy?" I reply, "We coaches are simple people; we just support our clients and hold them accountable." They laugh — they think I'm joking. I'm not. It's exactly what the best therapists also do — with one hand tied behind their backs, bound as they are by their need to diagnose and treat and the demands of a profession in which mental disorders are not discerned but created.

What about Antidepressants?

You may be thinking, "But don't antidepressants prove that depression does exist? I mean, when you treat an illness with a drug and you get better, doesn't that prove that you were ill in the first place?"

No, it doesn't.

To begin with, whether or not antidepressants actually work is open to debate. The very definition of what constitutes antidepressant effectiveness sets the bar very low. The physician Mark Hyman explained: "Just because antidepressants are popular doesn't mean they're helpful. Unfortunately...most patients taking antidepressants either don't respond or have only partial response. In fact, success is considered just a 50 percent improvement in half of depressive symptoms. And this minimal result is achieved in less than half the patients taking antidepressants. That's a pretty dismal record."

Second, drug companies regularly suppress research demonstrating the ineffectiveness of the antidepressants they sell, thus producing an inflated sense of their effectiveness. One example of this widespread practice is the following, as reported in *NewsInferno*: "Reboxetine, an antidepressant sold by Pfizer...is ineffective, and could even be harmful, according to a new study conducted by German researchers....Researchers from the German Institute for Quality and Efficiency in Health Care have accused Pfizer of failing to disclose negative clinical trial results for reboxetine, after finding that eight out of 13 significant trials were never published."

Third, the extremely high relapse rate after patients discontinue antidepressants suggests that *effectiveness* is being defined as the temporary alleviating or masking of symptoms. Sharon Begley reported in the *Wall Street Journal*: "Unless patients continue taking the drugs, they have a considerable risk of suffering a relapse in the year after they stop....A large 2001 study found that the risk of relapse in patients taking antidepressants only, in the year after they stop, is 80 percent. In contrast, patients receiving only cognitive behavior therapy in that study had a relapse rate of 25 percent in the year after ending treatment."

Fourth, multiple studies indicate that a large component of drug effectiveness may be the placebo effect. Maia Szalavitz wrote in *Time* magazine: "A small but vocal minority of researchers have also questioned whether the mood-enhancing benefit of antidepressants amounts to anything more than a psychological artifact. They point to studies that suggest the drugs' seemingly powerful effects are the same as those of a sugar pill. Most recently, a headline-grabbing *Journal of the American Medical Association* paper published in January [2010] found that antidepressants worked no better than a placebo in patients with mild or moderate depression."

John Kelley in *Scientific American* elaborated on this:

> In clinical practice, many people suffering from depression improve after taking antidepressants. But the evidence indicates that much of that improvement is a placebo response. Antidepressants do work in the sense that many patients in clinical practice show substantial improvement. However, if the standard is efficacy in comparison to placebo, the best available scientific evidence suggests that antidepressants do not work very well. Given their cost and side effects, the psychiatric community and the general public should not be satisfied with antidepressant medications that provide only a marginal benefit over placebo.

The fact that antidepressants are now prescribed for a myriad of very different "ailments" further suggests that we are looking at a placebo rather than a chemical effect. Peter Breggin wrote in *Talking Back to Prozac*:

> While Prozac was originally approved for depression — and only recently for obsessive-compulsive disorder — it and the other SSRIs quickly began to be prescribed for a wide variety of ailments and difficulties, such as seasonal affective disorder (SAD) or "winter blues," obesity, anorexia, bulimia, phobia, anxiety and panic disorder, chronic fatigue syndrome, premenstrual syndrome (PMS), post-partum depression, drug and alcohol addiction, migraine headaches, arthritis, body dysmorphic disorder (BBD), and, finally, behavioral and emotional problems in children and adolescents.

Wow.

There are more reasons than these to suspect the effectiveness of antidepressants. But even if it were proven to everyone's satisfaction that antidepressants work to "relieve the symptoms of depression," would that constitute proof that depression is a mental disorder? Hardly. All it would prove is that chemicals have effects and that they can alter a human being's experience of life.

Is that news?

Chemicals can make you giddy, they can cause you to hallucinate, they can give you an adrenaline rush, they can make you forget your troubles, they can give you an erection, they can cause you to skip your period. Chemicals can affect how your mind works. Chemicals can affect how you sleep. Chemicals can alter your moods. That a chemical, an antidepressant, can change your mood in no way constitutes proof that you have a mental disorder called depression. All that it proves is that chemicals can have an effect on mood.

There is a fundamental difference between taking a drug because it is the appropriate treatment for a medical illness and taking a drug because it can have an effect. This core distinction is regularly obscured in the world of treating depression. The mental health industry routinely makes the leap from "We don't know what you have and we *surely* don't know what's causing it" to "Take this chemical." This leap has naturally confused a lot of smart, sensible people who are not informed enough to ask, "Are you prescribing this drug because I have a biological disorder, or are you prescribing this drug because it is known to have an effect on my symptoms?"

An antidepressant may elevate your mood and rid you of symptoms. You may desperately want those positive effects and opt for chemicals to deliver them. You would need to factor in the characteristic side effects of antidepressants — among them sexual dysfunction, fatigue, insomnia, loss of mental abilities, nausea, and weight gain — and make your informed decision. To the extent that the chemicals really do deliver those effects and to the extent that their side effects aren't worse than their positive effects, antidepressants may be a reasonable choice. It certainly wouldn't be the first time someone took a chemical to get a respite from human unhappiness. But the fact that antidepressants can provide this respite does not constitute proof that they are a "treatment for a mental disorder called depression." *It is only proof that chemicals have effects.*

What Does Psychotherapy Prove?

The phrase *mental disorder* is supposed to put you in mind of medicine; and antidepressants, by their very existence, are supposed to constitute proof that a disorder, with a biological cause, exists. Let's say that you agree with me that giving something a name and providing chemicals that have an effect on that something do not constitute proof that you have a genuine disorder. However, you may still feel that something is going on that warrants that "mental disorder" label and that maybe that something is psychological rather than biological.

I'm afraid that emperor is also naked. It is no more legitimate to call an array of unwanted experiences a psychological disorder than it is to call it a mental disorder. It is the same specious operation. For it to represent something legitimate, the term *psychological disorder* would need to mean something more than experiences or feelings that are unwanted, unacceptable, odd, or extreme.

The two primary treatment methods that have arisen to treat mental disorders are chemicals (antidepressants) and talk (psychotherapy). Recently a great deal of investigative energy has gone into debunking the rationale for and efficacy of the chemical approach (see books such as *The Emperor's New Drugs,*

The Myth of the Chemical Cure, and *Anatomy of an Epidemic*). Psychotherapy, however, has largely escaped similar scrutiny. Probably the main reason is that it can work rather well — except not as a "treatment" for the "mental disorder of depression." Rather, it works because the right kind of talk can help reduce a person's experience of unhappiness.

Since there are no mental disorders to be treated, what is going on in psychotherapy? Chatting and relating. A human interaction is occurring that is just like the human interaction that occurs between two friends, when one friend is perhaps a little more psychologically savvy than the other. It isn't fair to call the kind of talk that happens between a psychotherapist and her client "just talk," since this talk can help enormously. But it also isn't sensible to put this talk on a pedestal. Thomas Szasz, who for fifty years has heroically exposed the mental health industry in books such as *The Myth of Mental Illness*, *The Manufacture of Madness*, and *The Medicalization of Everyday Life*, says:

> When I suggest that psychotherapy is a myth I do not mean to deny the reality of the phenomena to which that term is applied. People do suffer from all sorts of aches and pains, fears and guilts, depressions and futilities; many such persons do consult, or are compelled to consult, experts called psychotherapists; and one or more of the participants in the resulting transaction may consider it helpful, useful, or "therapeutic." The coming together of these two parties and the results of their coming together are conventionally called psychotherapy. All that exists and is very much a part of our social reality.

As Szasz explains, the myth is not that a troubled person arrives at the office of another person, sits with that person, talks to that person, and is sometimes helped by their conversation. Rather, the myth is that a fancy, scientific, medical-seeming thing that goes by the name of "psychotherapy" and purports to be the "treatment of mental disorders" is happening. Indeed, one proof that what has transpired is "talk" and not the "treatment of a mental disorder" is how little interest psychiatrists take in it. If psychotherapy were one of only two treatment methods that you believed worked to treat something, and if you were qualified to practice that something, why wouldn't you practice it? The fact is, psychiatrists rarely do.

In *Unhinged* psychiatrist Daniel Carlat recounts his experience treating a patient and suddenly realizing that he had done nothing "doctor-like" with her except write a prescription. He hadn't examined her; he hadn't asked for any medical tests. This realization that he wasn't acting like a genuine doctor was immediately followed by a second realization: that he also hadn't engaged in anything like psychotherapy with her. He wondered why he hadn't:

> Just as striking to me as the lack of typical doctorly activities in psychiatry is the dearth of psychotherapy. Most people are under the misconception that an appointment with a psychiatrist will involve counseling, probing questions, and digging into the psychological meanings of one's distress. But the psychiatrist as psychotherapist is an endangered species. In fact, according to the latest data from a group of researchers at Columbia University, only one out of every ten psychiatrists offers therapy to all their patients. Doing psychotherapy doesn't pay well enough. I can see three or four patients per hour if I focus on medications (such psychiatrists are called "psychopharmacologists"), but only one patient in that time period if I do therapy.

Carlat's is the usual reason given as to why few psychiatrists bother to talk with their patients, namely, that it is more profitable not to talk. But as real a reason is that the game they are playing doesn't require it. If in your bones you know that psychotherapy is as suspect a methodology as psychopharmacology — if, that is, you know that you are dealing with human unhappiness and not a mental disorder, then there is no good reason to waste time playing the talking game. Let all those people with their family therapist licenses and their love of talking talk! Let me play just one game — the quicker, more profitable one.

Countless studies have shown that "successful therapeutic outcomes" in therapy are related to the therapist's warmth — not the therapist's theoretical orientation, not her training, not her experience. This is exactly what we would expect. Clients most enjoy and most benefit from talking with someone they experience as a human being. They are talking about their human troubles and having a human interaction. If psychotherapy is the "talking cure," it is in exactly the same sense that chatting with a wise friend is a talking cure.

Prospective coaching clients sometimes ask me, "What will we be doing?" My answer is always the same: "We'll talk." That answer hardly satisfies them! They are looking for a professional-sounding pitch that justifies paying good money. I prefer not to provide them with that pitch. Often I'll relent a bit and explain what we'll be talking about. But first I want to make it very clear that essentially we are just talking.

That talking improves one's mood is not proof of the existence of a mental disorder called depression. It helps many people — perhaps most people — to talk about their problems, get advice, act on that advice, feel intimate with another person, and feel supported by another person. This is the help that psychotherapy at its best provides. Psychotherapy is sometimes effective because talking can help.

CHAPTER 3

FIFTEEN REASONS WHY PEOPLE BELIEVE THAT "DEPRESSION" EXISTS

GIVEN THE FACTS described in the previous discussion, why are so many millions of unhappy people so strongly attached to the idea that they have a mental disorder called depression? Why do they accept the idea that a mental disorder called depression even exists? Let's examine the reasons and revisit some of the points I've been making.

1. There is a culture-wide, almost worldwide, acceptance that depression is a mental disorder. Isn't this acceptance proof of its existence?

No. There is certainly a phenomenon. But for the phenomenon to be a disease or a disorder, it must be a disease or a disorder. That something needs remediating or changing doesn't make it a disease or a disorder. The fundamental linguistic game played by the mental health industry is to characterize anything that even remotely needs remediating or changing a disorder. That hundreds of millions of people agree to play this game only proves the power of naming.

2. We see depression everywhere. It is epidemic. Isn't the fact that we see it everywhere and that so many people are suffering from it proof of its existence?

No. What we see are a great many unhappy people, some mildly unhappy and some profoundly unhappy, who have naively or pointedly adopted the language of the mental health industry and who are willing or eager to characterize their unhappiness as this thing called a mental disorder. What we see is a great deal of unhappiness. We do not see depression unless we play the mental health industry's naming game.

3. Since mental health professionals say that such a disorder exists, mustn't it exist?

No. Mental health professionals once said that women who didn't want to be subjugated by their husbands were hysterical. Just a few short years ago mental health professionals said that homosexuality was a mental disorder. Mental disorders come into existence by virtue of a handful of people in a room deciding that a phenomenon ought to be called a mental disorder. Once this naming occurs and is codified, the rest of the profession goes along with the naming, and the general population follows. A group of people sitting in a room and deciding that certain human phenomena ought to be designated mental disorders doesn't make those phenomena mental disorders.

4. Isn't the fact that countless books, articles, websites, and guests on talk shows say that such a disorder exists proof that it exists?

No. Virtually none of the people who use the word *depression*, whether in connection with their own depression or that of others, have investigated whether the phenomenon they are talking about should be more properly thought of as a mental disorder or as profound unhappiness. They are simply parroting words and constructs provided by the mental health industry. That countless people use a word isn't proof that the word means what the creators of the word say it does. It only means that the word has become the shorthand — and in this case the incorrect and inappropriate — label for a phenomenon.

5. Isn't the fact that countless people assert that they know what un-happiness feels like and they know what depression feels like, and that they are certain that the two are completely different things, proof that depression is a mental disorder?

No. They are certainly experiencing one state as different from another. One person expressed the difference this way: "Where sadness makes you feel raw and skinless, depression is like wearing a snow suit and mittens and wondering why you can't feel the caress of life." However, that something feels worse than something else or different from something else isn't proof that it's a mental disorder. Riding a roller coaster feels very different from rocking on your porch, but the former isn't a disorder just because it turns your stomach and makes you scream.

6. Since drugs exist for the treatment of depression, doesn't it make sense to presume that it's a medical condition?

No. Chemicals have effects. That a certain chemical has a certain effect isn't the slightest proof that it is treating a disorder. Imagine a rampaging elephant loose in a village. You can down it with a tranquilizer dart, but does that mean that you've "treated" its "rampaging disorder"? No. You simply used a chemical to produce an effect.

7. Since it is treatable, mustn't it follow that it is some sort of medical condition?

No. The word *treatment* as used by the mental health industry is part of a naming game and has neither a medical nor a commonsense meaning. With regard to mental disorders, the word *treatment* doesn't mean "the helpful things you do after you have accurately identified the causes of a problem." A medical doctor treating an illness orders this treatment versus that one based on her understanding of what is causing the illness or her hypothesis about what might be causing it. A mental health professional asserts, without blushing or blinking an eye, that he has no clue what is causing your disorder but that he is nevertheless happy to treat it. This is an illegitimate use of the word *treatment* and would never pass muster in a hospital examination room.

8. Mustn't there be all sorts of scientific evidence that there is a mental disorder called depression?

No. Nor can there be, because first we would need a definition of mental disorder that was not specious. What scientific evidence could prove that your boredom, say, was a mental disorder? That some part of your brain didn't light up when you were bored? That some hormone got secreted when you were bored? That some neural transmitter functioned in some unusual way when you were bored? All of that would only be evidence that you were bored, not proof of a mental disorder. It is impossible to find scientific evidence to prove that a certain common human experience is a mental disorder unless you engage in fraudulent science.

9. Since medical tests are sometimes ordered, mustn't it follow that doctors are looking for the causes of a real disorder or verification of the existence of it?

No. Medical tests such as blood tests are not used to diagnose depression. Rather, they are used to identify or to eliminate from consideration organic problems (for example, central nervous system tumors, head traumas, multiple sclerosis, syphilis, hypothyroidism, or various cancers) known to cause the symptoms of depression or to exacerbate the symptoms of depression. For example, if you present insomnia as a symptom, there are tests to see if the insomnia might be related to some organic problem. Running this sort of test is not the same thing as "testing for depression."

10. Since there is compelling evidence that the brain actually changes its shape when a person is severely depressed and that parts of it can even atrophy, isn't that proof that depression is a mental disorder?

No. Let's say that you sit on your couch for a few months straight. You would expect to feel weaker. Would you call that weakness a disorder, or would you call it the natural result of sitting on your couch for a few months straight? That a body part begins to weaken and atrophy from a lack of use should be credited to its lack of use, not to a disorder. The fact that there is an observable biological event doesn't prove — or even imply — the presence of a disorder.

11. Maybe depression isn't a biological disorder, but don't we have ample proof of the existence of a psychological disorder called depression?

No. What would constitute a psychological disorder? First, you would need a definition of *psychological disorder* that wasn't specious. Such a definition would need to do more than assert that certain unwanted experiences, grouped together, amounted to an illness. Second, you would need sensible ways of distinguishing between normal human experience and whatever it is you'd defined as a psychological disorder. Third, you would need to mount treatments that addressed the causes you identified and not just the symptoms. None of that currently happens — nor could it ever legitimately happen as long as the thing being pathologized was ordinary human experience.

12. Because psychological tests can distinguish between depressed people and those who aren't depressed, doesn't that prove that the mental disorder of depression exists?

No. A psychological test asks you questions about your life experiences. In essence, a psychological test is a certain kind of self-report. You might, for example, indicate that you were sleeping poorly, that life held little interest for you, and that you were overeating. Then the game would be on: the more vivid a picture you painted of unhappiness, the higher your "depression score" would be. Self-reports can certainly distinguish between happier and unhappier people. But to say that you have "tested for depression" makes no sense.

13. If your circumstances improve and you don't feel less depressed, or if nothing in particular is going wrong and you still feel depressed, doesn't that prove that what you're experiencing must be a disorder?

No. You can be unhappy even though your circumstances are excellent. You can grow unhappy just because a cloud passed across the sun and you were reminded of your own mortality. To grow unhappy even though "objectively" all is well isn't proof of a disorder. It is only a completely understandable feature of human existence. Unhappiness can arise even at the moment when you feel happiest as you catch a whiff of nothingness or lament that this happiness is bound to prove fleeting. That you might feel unhappy even when the sun is shining is no proof of a mental disorder called depression.

14. If what I'm experiencing isn't a mental disorder, shouldn't I be able to just cheer up?

No. Your unhappiness may be pernicious. Your unhappiness may have many causes. You may view life through a lens that turns everything gray. That it may be possible to "cheer up" is very different from supposing that it should only take a snap of your fingers. And what is that "should" supposed to connote, anyway? No one can arbitrate your happiness or unhappiness. That you can't easily improve your mood or that you have no interest in improving your mood proves nothing about your mood being a mental disorder called depression.

15. Well, but something is going on, isn't it?

Yes. Of course *something* is going on. A lot of human unhappiness is going on. That something is going on doesn't prove the existence of a mental disorder called depression. Maybe you want to hand off the problem of your unhappiness to the putative experts. That desire is understandable. Maybe it embarrasses you to admit that you're profoundly unhappy when your unhappiness doesn't seem justified by your circumstances. That embarrassment is understandable. Maybe you find it hard to admit that life has turned out to be a cheat. That reluctance is understandable. Maybe you have all sorts of reasons for preferring to believe that your unhappiness is a mental disorder called depression. All those pressing and poignant reasons notwithstanding, it is not.

I hope I've convinced you that it is human sadness that is plaguing tens of millions of people and not "the mental disorder of depression." The natural question to ask next is, "What can be done to alleviate that sadness?" The rest of this book will provide answers to that question.

PART TWO

YOUR EXISTENTIAL PLAN

CHAPTER 4

THE EXISTENTIAL IDEAL — AND ITS REALITY

TENS OF MILLIONS OF PEOPLE are regularly unhappy. Maybe it's hundreds of millions. Maybe it's billions.

Why should that be surprising?

It makes no sense to suppose that a creature with consciousness could always feel happy. It is absurd and telling that as a society we think that unhappiness is an embarrassing, inappropriate emotion. It is so preposterous an idea that it should be laughed right out of the room. Yet somehow we have landed in this strange place where we are supposed to smile and smile, and if for a few weeks on end we can't make ourselves smile, then we have a mental disorder.

How can you be happy as you contemplate a billion people starving to death during a never-ending drought? Yes, you can find a way not to be conscious of that starvation — but then you aren't conscious of it. If you *are* conscious of it, should you also be feeling happy? Shouldn't that horror *make you feel unhappy?*

How can you be happy if you *are* one of those billion people?

How can you be happy as you watch your parents grow infirm, incontinent, and incoherent? Yes, you can avoid visiting them, caring for them, or thinking about them. But if you *are* visiting them, caring for them, and thinking about them, should you also be feeling happy? Shouldn't their predicament *make you feel unhappy?*

How can you be happy if you *are* one of those infirm parents?

How can you be happy if you've married someone you no longer love or even like? Shouldn't living a loveless life in the company of someone you don't want to know *make you feel unhappy?*

How can you be happy if you had a beautiful dream to make use of your brains and your spirit and you find yourself doing dumb, dispiriting work? Shouldn't living a life significantly short of the one you envisioned for yourself *make you feel unhappy?*

How can you be happy if you are obliged to spend 50, 60, or 70 percent of your waking hours doing work that does nothing but allow you to survive? Shouldn't being reduced to being a workhorse *make you feel unhappy?*

Sometimes we're unhappy with ourselves. We may be unhappy that we aren't doing enough, that what we're managing to accomplish doesn't rise to a sufficient level of excellence, that our behavior is out of control, that we've made decisions we now regret. This unhappiness may make you toss and turn at night as your mind races, which leads to chronic insomnia, which makes you more tired than usual — and more irritable and more unhappy too. *Sometimes we get very unhappy with ourselves.*

Sometimes we're unhappy with others. Maybe we're unhappy that our parents ignored or belittled us. Maybe we don't understand why some people are getting ahead and we aren't. Maybe we're unhappy with our mate for being colder and more unsupportive than we would wish him or her to be, unhappy with our boss for piling duties on our head, unhappy with that gallery owner for smirking when we showed him our paintings. This unhappiness may be on our minds so much that we have trouble concentrating on anything except our feelings of envy and betrayal. *Sometimes we get very unhappy with others.*

Sometimes we're unhappy with our circumstances. Maybe we feel trapped by the incessant need to pay this insurance premium and that car repair bill, trapped by a winter that lasts too long and a bank account too small to allow us to run off to somewhere sunny. Maybe we feel trapped by a life that sounds all right in the expressing but that feels dark, stressful, and ordinary in the living. Maybe feeling trapped this way makes us feel helpless, hopeless, sour, and irritable. *Sometimes we get very unhappy with our circumstances.*

Sometimes we're unhappy with life itself, with the idea that we come and go and do not really matter in the scheme of things. We're unhappy that there is no line of thought that ends anywhere except with a sense of the void. This anger at the hand you've been dealt, the hand that your species has been dealt — of consciousness of our own mortality and futility — can make us bored, listless, careless, short-tempered, and unhappy. *Sometimes we get very unhappy with life itself.*

I say none of this in a spirit of pessimism.

There is indeed a pessimistic tradition that argues that unhappiness is not just unavoidable but our species' dominant experience. In that tradition unhappiness is viewed as always nipping at our heels, threatening to overwhelm us with despair. One of the reasons that psychotherapists are so comfortable seeing depression everywhere is that the founding father of psychoanalysis, Sigmund Freud, was a major figure in the pessimist tradition. Freud argued that while our wishes can be beautifully fulfilled in fantasy, they can never be adequately fulfilled in reality. That discrepancy colors all of life. Given its profit motive and its theoretical orientation, no wonder the field of psychotherapy sees life as enveloped in darkness!

Joshua Dienstag, discussing this tradition in *Pessimism: Philosophy, Ethic, Spirit*, wrote: "From [the perspective of Freud and Schopenhauer], it is not really surprising that our experience is dominated by unhappiness. Our situation is out-of-joint with the universe to begin with. We cannot hope to set it right — we can only await the release from this predicament provided by death. In the meantime, we merely manage our condition — such management is, to Schopenhauer, the purpose of philosophy; for Freud, it is psychotherapy that serves this end. But the aim, in both cases, is not to create happiness or virtue but to minimize unhappiness."

To acknowledge the reality of unhappiness is not to assert the centrality of unhappiness. In fact, it is just the opposite. By taking the common human experience of unhappiness out of the shadows and acknowledging its existence, we begin to reduce its power. At first it is nothing but painful to say, "I am profoundly unhappy." The words cut to the quick. They seem to come with a life sentence and allow no room for anything sweet or hopeful. But the gloom can lift. It may lift of its own accord — or it may lift because you have a strong existential program in place whereby you pay more attention to your intentions than to your mood. I'll present such a program in a moment.

Let us be mature and truthful and accept the reality of unhappiness. It is not *the* coloration of life, but it is certainly one of life's colors. Moments of unhappiness happen. Days of unhappiness happen. Unhappiness can cloud a year or a decade. This does not make you "disordered," and it is nothing you should feel embarrassed about. Ah, but what to do? For the experience of unhappiness is not one you want to prolong or, if you can help it, repeat. The answer: Work your existential program. Let me present that program now.

The Existential Ideal

One way to deal with the inevitability of unhappiness is to lead a life based on existential ideals. You take as much control as possible of your thoughts, your attitudes, your moods, your behaviors, and your very orientation toward life and you turn your innate freedom into a virtue and a blessing.

That was a mouthful — and perhaps not really very plausible. Can people really take such control of life and master themselves that well?

It certainly doesn't seem so. The existential ideal has fallen pretty flat in the real world. Existentialism is an ambitious philosophy that demands that each human being try. It begs the individual to make use of the measure of freedom she possesses, to look life in the eye and deal with reality, and to stand tall as an advocate for human dignity. It argues that life, by pairing tremendous ordinariness with tremendous difficulty and by leading to nothing but death, is a cheat. And it argues that human beings can nevertheless cheat the cheater by adopting an indomitable attitude and making the meaning they require. This agenda sets the bar very high and doesn't seem to suit most people.

Existentialists such as Dostoyevsky, Nietzsche, Kafka, Sartre, and Camus themselves often failed at living with the bar set so high. They could beautifully articulate why the bar ought to be set there, at a place of personal responsibility and ethical action they called authentic living, but they found it inconveniently difficult to live that mindful, measured, and pure a life. They proved in the living that our foibles trump our resolutions much of the time. They proved it by womanizing. They proved it by gambling. They proved it by succumbing to addiction. They proved it by giving in to despair and taking to the sofa. They proved it by rejecting real work and choosing second-rate projects.

It was simply too hard to live as carefully, ethically, and authentically as the tenets of existentialism demanded. The tenets were lovely, albeit in an ice-water sort of way, but the reality was daunting. Therefore, existentialism never really caught on. For a while after the Second World War millions of young people read about it and nodded in agreement with its premises but drifted away from it because of its rigors. Jobs called; sex called; vision quests called; soccer on Saturday called; stock portfolios called. It was fine to read a little Nietzsche in college — but more sensible to put that behind you and get on with your commute.

Existentialism did not allow for an array of things that human beings actually wanted, such as permission to be petty and permission to waste vast amounts of time. It didn't condone spiritual enthusiasms, silent acquiescence, or slogan-size commandments. It frowned on group allegiance and social frivolity. Existential philosophy acknowledged these desires perhaps more clearly than any other philosophy but then asked people not to indulge them — and people passed.

People passed for other reasons too. Not only did existentialism demand that they live an ethically vigilant life in which each action was the culmination of an internal moral debate, but they were also supposed to transcend personality and the facts of existence and escape the net in which every human being is tangled. This was not only a lot to ask; it was perhaps unfair and impossible. How were you supposed to not be the person you had developed into? How were you supposed to shrug off illness, war, disaster, and every manner of calamity and constraint? Was any of that really doable?

To take one example, people were supposed to transcend pride. But our smartest, most talented people have rarely been able to come close to such maturity. In their relationship with each other, Dostoyevsky and Tolstoy couldn't. Camus and Sartre couldn't. Freud and Jung couldn't. Picasso and Matisse couldn't. Scientists haven't, businesspeople haven't, and parents attending Little League games or PTA meetings haven't. It turns out that egotistic, wounded pride isn't a snap to transcend. Wherever did we get the idea that it was?

Or take appetite. People with large, undeniable, and maybe unquenchable appetites — for sex, for peanuts, for experience, for seduction, for fast rides, for competition, for the rush of adrenaline — were supposed to put their appetites in their back pockets and approach life with the measured restraint of an ascetic. Authenticity required that you avoid gluttony, promiscuity, cruelty, and unnecessary danger. Who wanted to give any of those things up? Could they even *be* given up?

Or take human energy itself. In the existential vision human beings are in control of themselves. But what if you are flying along in a perfectly lovely manic way in pursuit of some dream and really don't want to stop and take a measured reckoning? What if you want to act impulsively — intuitively, if you like — and skip the stolid calm that would seriously slow you down? It seems as if a choice has to be made between snail-pace rationality and our very life force — and people choose pulsation over calculation.

To be fair, existentialists understood all this very well. Each danced the poignant dance of demanding much from human beings while doubting that the effort was possible or even plausible. They doubted and wondered. Why make such a Herculean effort at authenticity when personality hung like a lead weight around our necks and the facts of existence ruined so many of our plans? All that wondering and doubting led to those trademarks of existential thought: fear and trembling, nausea, existential anxiety, existential dread, and, of course, absurdity.

Given all this, the existential program that I'm about to present as the best way to deal with human unhappiness may appeal to you in the reading but may prove too difficult in the implementing — may prove even impossible. We are not as courageous or capable as existential thinkers claim we are or wish we were, nor can we do an even adequate job of transcending the pitfalls of personality, negotiating the facts of existence, and living maturely. So working this arduous existential program may prove out of reach.

Or maybe it won't. Maybe you'll find authentic living suitable and doable. Let's champion that hope! If you would like to try to live that strange, shining ideal — an authentic life — given all the hard and perhaps impossible demands it will make on you, what follows is a program for doing so. I think you'll recognize it as what you've been searching for and as the best answer to the problem of human unhappiness.

Your Existential Program

To paraphrase an old joke, if you put two existentialists in a room you'll end up with three opinions. Even about the most fundamental questions, for instance about whether or not something called "spirit" or "god" exists, there will likely be no agreement. If it were possible to tease out the place where existentialists agree the most about fundamentals, it would probably sound like the following, from Maurice Friedman's *The Worlds of Existentialism*: "There is a crucial and inescapable distinction between authentic and inauthentic existence. Man's task in life is to authenticate his existence, and to the existentialist this can never mean the mere adherence to external moral codes, on the one hand, or the romantic's deification of passion and feeling, on the other, nor even on the vitalist's emphasis on the organic flow of life. Instead it means personal choice, decision, commitment, and ever again that act of valuing in the concrete situation that [which] verifies one's truth by making it real in one's own life."

The following existential program is designed to help you "verify your truth by making it real in your own life" and to support you in eliminating the unhappiness that comes from inauthentic living. Not all unhappiness will vanish if you follow this program; you're a human being, after all, and not immune to pain. But a lot of your unhappiness will..

This existential program emphasizes the existential, the cognitive, and the behavioral. Living authentically means organizing your life around your answers to three fundamental questions. The first is, "What matters to you?" The second is, "Are your thoughts aligned with what matters to you?" The third is, "Are your behaviors aligned with what matters to you?" The following are the elements of the program. In subsequent chapters we'll examine each in turn.

You Look Life in the Eye

You begin by removing the protective blinders that human beings put in place to avoid noticing the many painful facts of existence, including painful facts about their personality shortfalls. This unblinkering brings life into stark relief, and after that first gasp, life as it is can finally be faced and accepted.

You Investigate Meaning

You decide to understand "what meaning means" so that you can proceed to lead your life in ways that feel meaningful to you. You single out meaning as the one thing you really need to understand, realizing that if you do not fathom it you will likely remain confused about and estranged from life.

You Decide to Matter

You recognize that the universe is not built to care about you. *You* must care about you. You must announce that you have decided to matter. You must announce that you are making the startling, eye-opening decision to take responsibility for your thoughts and your actions and to lead life instrumentally.

You Accept Your Obligation to Make Meaning

You finally let go of the demoralizing wish that meaning rain down on you from on high and accept that the only meaning that exists is the meaning that you make. You announce once and for all that you are the final arbiter of your life's meaning.

You Decide How to Matter

Once you accept your obligation to make meaning, your next task is to decide how to proceed. Is there some step-by-step meaning-making process available, or is it much more a speculative, seat-of-the-pants sort of thing? Or maybe it revolves around honoring a single principle — and if so, can you name it?

You Honor Your Wants, Needs, and Values

You take a smart view of the human predicament and recognize that while you want to honor the values you deem worthy, life presents you with other purposes and pleasures too, among them guilty ones. You wisely factor in satisfying your desires, boosting your ego, enduring drudgery — you factor in everything human as you plot your course.

You Create a Life-Purpose Vision

You aim your investigation in the direction of identifying and articulating your life purposes. You let go of the idea that life has "a" purpose and replace it with the idea that life comes with many purposes and that you get to decide which ones are yours. You create a life-purpose vision and remember it even when you are tired, bothered, distracted, upset, and otherwise not in your best frame of mind. When life resumes it habitual busyness, you still firmly hold your intentions and manifest them.

You Use Your Existential Intelligence

We are built to think about and to make meaning. One way to construe this innate ability is as "existential intelligence." However, it is one thing to possess existential intelligence and another thing to use it. You reduce your experience of unhappiness by employing your existential intelligence in the service of authenticity.

You Focus on Meaning Rather Than Mood

One decision that an existentially aware person makes is to focus on making meaning rather than on monitoring moods. If you pester yourself with the question, "How am I feeling?" you create unhappiness. If the question you pose yourself instead is, "Where should I invest meaning next?" you live more authentically.

You Snap Out of Trance

Forces within us propel us in the direction of personal trance, a self-protective state of haze and fog that we experience when we simply go through the motions. Moreover, societal forces manipulate us into buying whatever our culture is selling, whether it be designer shoes or patriotism, and push us into cultural trance. Both trance states must be resisted.

You Reckon with the Facts of Existence

The world is not built to accommodate you. Your favorite bakery may close, or war may break out — from the smallest to the largest, the facts of existence are exactly what they are. They include pain and pleasure, loyalty and betrayal, life and death. And they include your formed personality. All this you learn to navigate as best a human being can.

You Personalize a Vocabulary of Meaning

You support your efforts at authentic living by adopting words and phrases that allow you to communicate with yourself intelligibly. You use and champion phrases such as *making meaning* and *investing meaning* to firm up the commitment you've made to live in a clear-eyed, mindful, and intentional way.

You Incant Meaning

You marry the power of deep breathing with short phrases that support your intentions, and you create breath-and-thought bundles called "incantations" that calm and center you. These incantations — for example, "meaning is a wellspring" and "I interpret the universe" — become your affirmations in the realm of meaning.

You Maintain a Morning Meaning Practice

You start each day by creating an existential plan for that day by deciding where you intend to invest meaning and by identifying those parts of the day that you intend to hold as vacations from meaning. This practice, which takes just a few minutes (or even just a few seconds), orients you in the direction of daily meaning.

You Negotiate Each Day

A day is a dynamic affair made up of meaning-making efforts and vacations from meaning. You choose your meaning opportunities, you repair meaning when it gets torn, and you accept the tedious, unrewarding, difficult bits with practiced maturity. Each day is a project requiring existential engineering skills as you bridge your way from one meaningful experience to the next.

You Seize Meaning Opportunities

Certain human endeavors, among them love, creativity, service, self-actualization, and achievement, are regularly experienced as meaningful. By conceptualizing these activities and states of being as meaning opportunities, you remind yourself of just how much meaning is available to you.

You Handle Meaning Crises

You learn how to handle meaning crises, and when a meaning crisis strikes, you decide which of the several options available to you — getting a grip and making the best of it, initiating changes that alter and improve the situation, investing in new meaning opportunities, and so on — you'll employ to restore meaning.

You Engage in Existential Self-Care

Existential self-help consists of grounding yourself in a pair of realities: that life is exactly as it is and that you are obliged to keep your head up and make yourself proud. By accepting the realities of life and by asserting that you are the sole arbiter of the meaning in your life, you provide yourself with a sure footing as you actively make meaning.

You Engage in Cognitive Self-Care

We help ourselves make meaning and reduce our sadness by talking to ourselves in ways that support our intentions. We want our thoughts to provide us with hope, defuse our doubts, and settle our arguments with life. What we think is how we feel, and it is up to us to get a good grip on what we think.

You Engage in Behavioral Self-Care

You do not always have to do something "out in the world" in order to make meaning or to feel less sad. Sometimes the answer lies in simply adjusting your attitude or reframing the situation. But often you are obliged to do real things. Knowing when and how to act is an essential part of your existential program.

Even if you decide to take antidepressants or engage in psychotherapy to get help with your unhappiness, you will still have to find ways of dealing with your meaning needs, the shadows of your personality, your consciousness of mortality, and the facts of existence. The existential program that I've just outlined can help.

Hold it lightly !
You engage in Spiritual Selfcare
in Knowing MARA, your
gods-demons. conflicts & in
feeding them with your body. ?
A new understanding of the
Eucarist sacrament, from
ancient Tibetan Knowledge -
(Buddhism).
Hold it lightly! Everything
start with the pen.
How much energy? How lightly
@ this point in time? Now -Here.

CHAPTER 5

YOU LOOK LIFE IN THE EYE

I TRAIN MEANING COACHES and even they, with their clear stake in upholding the existential ideals of effort and personal responsibility and their fervent hope that clients will rise to the occasion and make personal meaning, tend to find the ideals of existentialism a bit punitive and perfectionistic. It seems to most people that, for example, when Darwin said, "For a man to waste even an hour of his time means that he doesn't understand the value of life," they are obliged to come back with, "That is setting the bar too high." Even people with an affinity for freedom do not take freedom to mean trying all the time.

The first step in our program, looking life in the eye, is likewise an idea that many people might want to reject. They may think that all that awareness will only bring increased suffering. Won't you suffer more if you admit that you are a hundred pounds overweight than if you deny it and blame your discomfort when you fly on the smallness of airplane seats? Won't you suffer more if you admit that you are correct in your suspicion that your parents never loved you than if you go on smiling at holiday meals and making excuses for their insults? Isn't denial the better policy?

It may be. Let's admit that the matter is an open question. It may prove less daunting and less painful to use your defenses and construct a world that resembles the real world but that is filtered so as to obscure unhappy truths from view. Rather than feel the full weight of your poverty, you drink, fight, and just live. Rather than speculate about the role you play in your lack of success, you smoke, shop, pop pills, and just live. Rather than admit that your ailments flow from your personality, you make appointments with your spiritual adviser, your personal trainer, and your Jungian analyst. That may be the way.

Looking life in the eye demands intellectual rigor. You have to work hard just to think clearly about the difference between things-in-themselves and our subjective experience of things, a branch of inquiry known as phenomenology. It is much easier to accept collective and conventional wisdom about how you are supposed to feel when you see a flower, a tank, a puppy, or a flag than to think through what you are really feeling. It is much easier to smile at a flower and salute a flag than it is to take your personal pulse and tease out your feelings, what with everyone smiling and saluting around you.

There is a long intellectual tradition of trying to understand the relationship between things-as-they-are and our experience of those things. You can walk through an arboretum and experience it as a lovely place, or you can take it as a shortcut home and feel nothing for its beds of flowers. In fact, its grasses may make you sneeze; it may remind you that some people are lucky enough to have time to stroll here, while you do not; it may annoy you that all of this acreage is devoted to flowers and not to housing for the homeless. The thing-as-it-is, the arboretum, is one thing, and our experience of it is another.

To look life in the eye is to look both at things-as-they-are and at our experience of those things. To look at one but not the other provides us with too little information about life's possibilities. An arboretum may objectively be a lovely place, but if it holds no meaning for you and actually angers you, it is not a lovely place *for you*. Yes, you might decide to change your mind and your feelings and learn to like arboretums. But to engage in work of that sort you would first need to know that your usual response to beds of flowers is to want them dismantled. This is not the kind of knowing that most people want.

There is the further real danger that by looking life in the eye you will conclude that it is very ordinary. How special do things appear when you peer behind the curtain and take a close look at them? How many heroes would fall off their pedestals if we learned their complete histories? Would we still clap wildly at the end of an action movie if we'd heard the director explain how he manipulated the audience into caring about his immoral characters? Wouldn't everything become more tawdry and ordinary if we looked at life too closely?

How special would life seem if we stared hard at it? We eat; we take care of our bodily functions; we make small talk with the people we encounter; we work one of the ordinary jobs that society creates to fill human needs; we run errands; we check our emails; we relax with a television show; we have a glass of wine with a friend; we root for the home team; we knit; we watch a movie; we pay the bills; we go to sleep. Isn't such a list almost a recipe for unhappiness?

We find it hard to admit the reality of ordinariness. The language of equality and of the human potential movement seduced people into believing that human life was by its nature special. Since most of life is not *experienced* as special, people grew sad, wondering why their existence, which was supposed to feel special, rarely felt that way. Indeed, if you want to maintain the feeling that life is special, shouldn't you avoid eyeing it too closely? Most people would say yes.

Nor is it just life that is ordinary. We ourselves are largely ordinary as well. Most of us have ordinary looks, an ordinary intelligence, an ordinary income, ordinary talents. Most people sing off-key. Few people scintillate in conversation. Few business meetings produce anything the least bit extraordinary. Not only is much of life routine and humdrum; we ourselves do not make the earth shake. How lovely is that information?

The existential ideal also demands that we look carefully at our motives. Well, if that isn't the last straw! Why in heaven's name would I want to know that I am volunteering not to be of service but to avoid being home alone with my husband? Why would I want to reveal to myself that I failed my children as much as they failed me? Why would I want to reveal my secrets to myself when by keeping them hidden I can boost my ego, improve my image, and give cover to my shadowy impulses?

So we turn away from looking. Every day books come out with titles that are the equivalent of *Everything Is Perfect!*, *The Present Moment Is Beautiful!*, *Be Happy No Matter What!*, and *Dream It and It Will Happen!* These are the books that many people crave. Why, then, should you look life in the eye if that scrutiny may increase your suffering, make trouble for you, or blow your cover? Well, because it is a more honest way of living. Equally important, it may turn out that you have wagered on the wrong horse and that you will actually experience less unhappiness with your eyes open than you would with your head in the sand.

What are some of the countless sources of human unhappiness? Two powerful ones are a loveless upbringing and feelings of helplessness. These are well-known "causes of depression." All you need to do to create the "symptoms of clinical depression" in animals is to withhold love in their childhoods or to make them feel helpless as adults. One or the other is sufficient. Of the many animal experiments that offer convincing proof of this, three famous ones stand out: Harry Harlow's "wire monkey" experiments, Joseph Brady's "executive monkey" experiments, and Martin Seligman's "shocked dog" experiments.

Feelings such as "I am not loved" or "I feel helpless" produce symptoms of clinical depression or, to say it correctly, profound unhappiness. Is it better to deny that you are feeling these things and remain depressed or to look life in the eye, admit to these feelings, cry bitter tears, and then get up and make a better life for yourself? So many people believe that not knowing is the better option and therefore keep their true feelings and their real understanding under wraps. Isn't it better to look those truths in the eye, feel the excruciating pain that may arise, and then go on to live?

Existential living requires awareness. Of course, this may prove a bad bet. It is hard to get awareness back in the bottle after it has been released. Therefore it is worth hesitating before embarking on the journey I'm describing. You may experience tremendous rewards by beginning to see clearly, but you may also get a painful eyeful. If you are willing to take this gamble, say yes, without any equivocations, clarifications, or addendums. The payoff may be a tremendous release of unhappiness right off the bat as you finally accept that life is what it is and that you are not exempt from reality.

You do not look life in the eye just for the sake of seeing clearly. You do not look life in the eye so that, like a swimmer jumping daily into freezing water, you can prove your hardiness. You do not look life in the eye so as to feel superior to your fellow blinkered human beings. You do it so that you can arrive at your own truth and make the best possible decisions about how you want to live. You take this gamble so that you can actively make life as meaningful as possible.

Meaning is completely subjective

CHAPTER 6

YOU INVESTIGATE MEANING

NOTHING IS MORE IMPORTANT than meaning, and nothing is so little investigated. Scores of branches of philosophy are devoted to subjects such as ontology and epistemology, and none to an investigation of meaning. As far as I know, in no class at any level of learning is meaning introduced as a subject of possible interest. It is never brought up in the diagnosing of mental disorders and only brought up in their treatment by the occasional existential psychotherapist. When it comes up at all, it is usually as an individual cry of anguish over the fact that meaning has gone missing.

Why is the thing that is most important to us also the thing that is least investigated? Because human beings find it painfully difficult to accept that meaning is only a subjective psychological experience. They want meaning to refer not to a psychological state, as it does, but to something real, solid, important, and larger than life. They would rather that meaning reside somewhere, even if they can't access that place or understand it, than to have it live right inside them as an artifact of existence. They fear that if meaning doesn't *mean something more* than subjective experience, then life is exactly as arbitrary, pointless, and paltry as they fear it is.

This fear is like a child's dread of the monster in the closet.

Every parent knows what to do about that fear. You turn on the light and open the closet door. If human beings are to rid themselves of the chronic unhappiness that comes from the paralyzing misconception that meaning is out there somewhere, all they need to do is turn on the light, open the closet door, and breathe a huge sigh of relief. Meaning is neither lost nor unavailable. It is waiting for us. All we need to do is think and act in ways that tease it out of its latency.

What you are teasing out is a certain psychological experience. Things do not have meaning; human beings experience meaning. Nothing is intrinsically meaningful or intrinsically not meaningful. Some endeavors, such as service, ethical action, and self-actualization, and some states of being, such as contentment, appreciation, and intimacy, are indeed regularly experienced as meaningful. A list of these meaning opportunities makes for an excellent "meaning menu" to peruse as you decide where you want to invest your human capital — and I'll provide such a menu in a subsequent chapter. But they are not intrinsically meaningful. They are only meaningful when they are *experienced as meaningful*.

Consider the following. Four men are riding in a car and pass a tree. For the first man, the tree holds no particular meaning. For the second man it has great meaning, since he carved his initials into this tree as a boy. It reminds him of a time when his loving parents were still alive, and he experiences it as an object of love and nostalgia. For the third man the tree possesses a certain amount of meaning, because its bark can cure rashes and he is a student of natural treatments. For him, it is an object of scientific interest. For the fourth man, the driver, it holds powerful meaning, because he has been contemplating suicide and has envisioned driving his car into a tree exactly like this one. For him, it is an object of awful attraction. The tree has no intrinsic meaning, but three of these men find it meaningful in various ways.

Or consider this. Four women sit knitting together. The first woman finds knitting meaningful because it is the one activity in which her husband doesn't intrude or lay down the law. For her, it is a sanctuary. The second woman finds knitting meaningful because she associates it with an ordered universe in which leaves turn colors in the autumn, children obey, and women knit. For her, it is a satisfying emblem of the way her life knits together. The third woman finds knitting meaningful because it has a social and political valence: it represents the choice she is making to value "women's work" over "patriarchal art gallery art." For her, it is an activist stance. The fourth woman, ordered by her husband to knit with these women because their husbands are his bosses, finds their gossip intolerable and the knitting boring. For her, knitting is a meaningless activity and these hours spent knitting a horror. Knitting has no intrinsic meaning, but three of these women find it meaningful, and for very different reasons.

Meaning — what we value, how we construe our life purposes, what we make of the facts of existence — is a completely subjective affair. To take another kind of example, it is neither objectively meaningful to explore space nor objectively meaningful not to explore space. You can make arguments on either side having to do with humankind's innate need to explore, the advantages to a nation that can wage war from outer space, the squandering of resources better spent on feeding and housing the poor, and so on. You can — and no doubt do — have an opinion about space exploration. But that is all there is: your personal opinion and the personal opinions of others. There is absolutely no objective truth about whether space exploration is or isn't meaningful, since there is no one in charge of meaning except each individual.

Meaning is private, personal, individual, and subjective. Every argument for the objectivity of meaning is merely someone's attempt to elevate his subjective experience and his opinions above yours and mine. Whether we do or do not go ahead with space exploration has nothing whatsoever to do with the innate meaningfulness of the endeavor, there being none, and everything to do with who gets to decide.

Whether you find it more meaningful to sit for an hour by a pond watching ducks paddle or more meaningful to hop up after two minutes and rush home to work on your screenplay is entirely your decision — and one that might change tomorrow. Who else but you could decide how you intend to order your values, manifest your ethics, and construe meaning? Likewise, who else but you is in a position to deal with the sometimes terrible-feeling shifts in meaning that can't help but occur? For your meanings will indubitably shift. Not only is meaning subjective; meanings are bound to shift and change.

Consider the following. On Monday, you pledge to get fit and take care of your body. On Tuesday, getting some devastating news about your son's health, you offer up one of your organs to save his life, putting your own body at risk. On Wednesday (some months later, having recovered from your operation), hearing troubling news about a threat to your country, you support your son's decision to enlist, even though enlisting constitutes a threat to his life, the life you recently gave one of your organs to save. On Thursday (of the following month), having learned more about the war, you protest your country's involvement and wish that your child could come back from that war — right now.

Each action you took came from a different meaning orientation. Each new orientation superseded and even flat-out contradicted the previous one. First, preserving your body was among your highest concerns and considerations; then, in the blink of an eye, it slipped to a place below a new value, that of saving your son's life. Yet very soon thereafter you accepted the proposition that, however much you valued his life, he had acted correctly in putting his life on the line in defense of his country. But the shifting didn't stop there. A month later that proposition no longer felt true, not with the war now appearing wrongheaded and corrupt. What happened? You hadn't just changed your mind each time. You hadn't just espoused a new opinion. You experienced earthquake-size subjective meaning shifts.

Meaning is subjective; it shifts and changes. Another of its singular features is that it isn't always needed! This is a wonderful fact of human existence. You do not need the psychological experience of meaningfulness all the time. Meaning is a necessity, but in the way that we need water and not in the way that we need oxygen. We need oxygen all the time, but we can store water and do not need to drink it every second. We can go for hours without drinking and not experience a "hydration deficit." Meaning is like that: you can follow a meaningful experience with a meaning vacation and not suffer any existential distress.

It is a mental mistake, one of the most unfortunate ones that you can make, to believe that you need meaning all the time. If you make that mistake, then you'll pine for meaning when it's absent and feel as if life is a cheat. Over time, this pining is bound to turn into chronic unhappiness. The second you realize that meaning can be treated like water and not oxygen, you can relax into a powerful new way of being: you make exactly as much meaning as you need and you let the rest of life hum along in the gear of meaning neutral.

CHAPTER 7

YOU DECIDE TO MATTER

HAVING LOOKED LIFE IN THE EYE and engaged in your own investigations of meaning you may begin to realize that you must take responsibility for your stake in the world, for your thoughts, for your behaviors, for your efforts at living ethically, and for your very orientation vis-à-vis life. You orient yourself around the idea that what you do matters to you, that *you* matter to you, even if the universe doesn't give a fig about you. You decide to matter, not as a grandiose king or queen (or as a two-year-old) defines mattering but as an ethical adult intent on living authentically matters. You make yourself proud by putting everything on the table.

Most people do not decide to matter in this way. Their petty squabbles matter to them; the service they receive in restaurants matters to them; whether their team wins or loses matters to them; where they will get their next drink matters to them; winning at the game of physical appearance or cards or business or sex matters to them. An infinite number of things matter to them — everything except their own efforts at authentic living. Most people seem to be ruled by their "selfish genes" as they defensively turn away from the daily heroism required of person intent on living authentically.

Paradoxically enough, much of their petty, prima

mattering is the result of the lessons they've received that they don't really matter. Countless people grow up being punished for attempting to matter. Their culture drills into them the idea that they are one of many and that the group comes first: their country, their religion, their clique, their block, people with last names like theirs, people with their skin color. Many life lessons teach them that it is wrongheaded, immoral, and dangerous to stand up as a voice of one. Rather than stand up, they engage in pettiness.

But the fact that people like to preen and easily fall into lockstep doesn't completely explain their genuine, bone-deep unwillingness to stand tall. Their difficulty in deciding to matter is not really explained by their selfish genes and by the many negative life lessons they have learned. The main obstacle to authentic living faced by a contemporary person is her belief that human life is basically meaningless. Any reasons that she tries to adduce for mattering are overwhelmed by the strong possibility, bordering on certainty, that she and her fellow human beings are only excited matter put on earth for no reason other than that the universe could do it. Life is mere pointless happenstance and not worth taking seriously.

This bitter pill is a new view, barely two hundred years old. Before that, life seemed special. For thousands of years the idea of life as categorically different from nonlife, unique and important in the cosmos, was a core tenet of natural philosophy. The idea of the uniqueness of life, a tenet of the philosophy known ___ ___. seemed compelling until biologists, beginning with ___ Wöhler, who accidentally synthesized urea ___ rganic compounds could be manufactured ___ erials. We can date our present difficulties ___ ntaining meaning from that single event — ___ rea. From that day forward a new philosophy was needed, since life had lost much of its mystery, sanctity, and glamour.

Once you join the scientific materialists, as all of us have done to a greater or lesser degree, and believe that you can make human beings simply by striking dead atoms with powerful but meaningless forces, life turns meaningless. This is the basic problem with which we've been wrestling for two centuries. To be sure, religions and spiritual beliefs are more popular than ever, and ancient vitalist arguments are still upheld in every church. But the suspicion that we do not matter continues to haunt us all.

We manage to bear up, despite the suspicion that we are merely excited matter. We find ways to bear up almost every day. But on some days we discover that we can't bear up; on those days we despair about our cosmic unimportance and grow furious with the facts of existence. We feel saddened and defeated and lose our motivation to make meaning. The very word *meaning* strikes our ears as a cosmic joke. Because we fear that we are merely excited matter and consequently hold a grudge against the universe, we feel lost and alienated.

Battered by these thoughts, a modern person is driven to throw up her hands and cry, "Why bother! Why wrestle this stupid novel into existence? I might as well find some simple pleasures, eat chocolate, take a bubble bath, and to hell with the idea of making meaning!" So she eats chocolate and takes a bubble bath. But within minutes she is forcibly struck by the counterthought that "meaning must have meaning." A countervailing energy arises in her, something like hope and something like pride, an energy that readies her to do combat with her sincere belief that she is utterly unimportant.

When people try to throw up their hands and resign themselves to accepting postmodern meaninglessness and the illusory nature of meaning, they often find that they can't. *Meaning* continues to vibrate in a way that convinces them that, while it may be a difficult and even suspect word, it is not an empty word. *Meaning* means something; and, as a consequence, an authentic life is possible. At the last instant, ready to embrace the terrible fruits of materialism, they return with a vengeance to the belief that a meaningful life can be led and that they are obliged to choose that way.

In our hearts, we opt for life. We opt to really live the twenty years or the sixty years ahead of us. This may be all that we have, but it is exactly what we have. As nineteenth-century philosopher Richard von Schubert-Soldern aphoristically put it, "To understand life, we must contrast it with death." We force life to mean because we are alive and not dead. We force life to mean until death releases us from our responsibility to live authentically. We say, "While I am alive, I can love." We say, "While I am alive, I can learn a few things." We say, "While I am alive, I can help in some ways." We say, "While I am alive, I can create." We live authentically because we can.

In the two decades after the Second World War, when the French existentialists Camus and Sartre were becoming internationally recognized figures and the philosophy dubbed existentialism was gaining millions of interested followers, it looked as if issues of personal freedom and meaning-making might become subjects of deep, abiding interest to people everywhere. But very quickly people retreated from existentialism's steely demands. Even those who had read every word written by the existentialists found it impossible to look life squarely in the eye and announce, "I am the final and complete arbiter of meaning. The only meaning my life can have is the meaning with which I invest it."

The most important shift for the contemporary person to make is the one demanded by the existentialists, the shift from the despairing "Why do I exist?" to the bracing "I exist." She must stop pestering herself with the unanswerable questions that plague her — the need to know why she is alive, what made the universe, who can teach her about the meaning of life, and what are the first or final causes — and accept as her mantra "I am alive."

In her aliveness she finds everything she needs to know about how to live. All she needs to do is accept her purest understanding of her own meaning-making responsibilities. She doesn't have to adapt to existence any more than a bird has to adapt to the sky. She and existence have already adapted together. She simply has to accept that she is the only possible maker of personal meaning. Part of her wants to cry out, "I don't belong here, there's no place for me here, the hell with it!" But she does belong here, and she must pull her chair up to the table.

Even if she manages to do this, some postmodern malaise will persist. In a corner of her mind, today's smart, sensitive person is always *this close* to believing that meaning is an illusion and that meaninglessness is the true state of affairs. The best she can do is inoculate herself against this potential loss of meaning, and consequent chronic unhappiness, by devoting another corner of her mind to the rejoinder that meaning is not an illusion and that her life can be made to mean. This is the dynamic, unavoidable tension that adds unwanted stress to every contemporary person's life: even as she is poised on the brink of meaninglessness, she must repeatedly fight her way back to meaning.

You take this postmodern coloration into account by refusing to entertain the idea that *meaning* is a meaningless word. *Meaning* may well not mean what we would like it to mean. It may only mean something like "that which my human nature elevates to a high status, even though that elevation is of no concern to the universe at large." It may only mean "a psychological state of a certain sort." Even if it means just that, then *meaning* has meaning for you. It may be a folly and a gamble to make this deal with yourself, to announce that "meaning means" and that it must mean until you cease to exist, but it is the only authentic game in town.

If we refuse to matter, our meaning-making efforts peter out and we end up settling for second-rate meaning substitutes or meaninglessness, each with its attendant unhappiness. But if we hold ourselves up to a lofty, entirely self-imposed standard — that we are determined to matter, in accordance with our highest principles — then we imbue our meaning-making efforts with the seriousness that we know they require.

Deciding to matter does not answer every meaning question. It alone will not make a boring meeting meaningful or a mistake that ruins a novel a pleasant experience. It alone will not keep meaning afloat on gloomy days when nothing feels worth attempting. It alone will not cure a hormonal imbalance or end an Arctic winter. Still, it is a vital step on the path to authentic living. Existential crisis management begins with the decision to matter.

We all face the postmodern question, "Do I or my efforts matter?" As psychologist and writer Irving Yalom put it, "How does a being who needs meaning find meaning in a universe that has no meaning?" At first glance there seems to be no answer to this terrible question. But the answer is straightforward. We have been given life. Part of our inheritance is human consciousness. Out of this human consciousness arises the idea that we can live righteously and meaningfully. Therefore, we can opt to do just that. Maybe we are trivial creatures in a trivial universe. Will you allow that suspicion — even that fact — to paralyze you? Or will you come back to mattering?

You decide to matter. When you decide to matter, suddenly many things matter *less*: that it is cloudy out, that your toast isn't buttered to your liking, that your mother continues to insult you. You no longer need to look a certain way, act a certain way, or defend the indefensible. You're less susceptible to the lure of news and gossip. All that shrinks to the size of the period at the end of this sentence. You accept the existentialist's dare and announce that your course is your course, even if it meets with the approval and the applause of no one. You decide to matter.

CHAPTER 8

YOU ACCEPT YOUR OBLIGATION
TO MAKE MEANING

WE ARE ON THE THRESHOLD of understanding a shining idea: that each individual life can have meaning, even if the universe has none. Each of us comes with appetites, genetic predispositions, and everything else that *human being* connotes, and still we are free to choose whatever meaning we intend to make. Nature has granted us this. I get to decide what will make me feel righteous and happy, and you get to decide what will make you feel righteous and happy. You can turn the meaning that was waiting to be made into the meaning of your life.

You, and you alone, are the sole arbiter of the meaning in your life. That is the awesome proposition facing every contemporary person. As limited as we are in a biological and psychological sense and as constrained as we are by the facts of existence, we are nevertheless existentially free. When we do not live that way, honoring that existential freedom, we grow sad. When we do not live that way, we find ourselves wishing that we had opted for authenticity and had decided to matter.

It isn't that people don't work hard or try hard. They do. But two thoughts — that they are disposable throwaways in a meaningless universe and that nothing they do can alter that painful truth — play havoc beneath the surface, draining them of motivation and causing them profound unhappiness. You must meet these doubts by announcing that meaning does not exist until you make it and by donning the mantle of meaning maker. The moment you do this, all previous belief systems, both those that told you what to believe and those that told you that there was nothing to believe, vanish.

People customarily address their meaning issues in one or another of several unfortunate ways. One way is to shrug their shoulders and to try to ignore the problem. This sounds like, "I don't know what 'meaning' means, and I'm not interested." A second way is to hunt for meaning as if it were a lost treasure. This sounds like, "I will know what life means once I get to the top of the mountain." A third way is to bow to the authority of others, abdicating personal responsibility. This sounds like, "I do what God says." A fourth way is to take a truth, that there is only subjective meaning, and run with it in the direction of unbridled self-interest. This sounds like, "Everything is permitted and I can do whatever I damn well please." A fifth way is to stare too long at the reality that we are merely excited matter and collapse in existential pain. This sounds like, "Nothing I do really matters, given my puny status in an indifferent universe."

These are the usual ways that people deal with their meaning issues. But these are all poor choices. There is a better way, better in the sense that it acknowledges your unwillingness to bury your head in the sand; honors your storehouse of experience, a storehouse that makes seeking unnecessary; matches your desire for freedom, a desire that renders obedience an obscenity; aligns with your desire to take ethical action and to live righteously, a desire that makes rationalizing selfishness intolerable; and agrees with your recognition of the pointlessness of pointlessness — your recognition that nihilism is simply not a sensible option. You reject these five options as unworthy, and you choose a sixth one: passionate meaning-making.

This is *the* crucial step of any existential program.

But it isn't that easy to announce, "I am a meaning maker." For many reasons, you may stop at the threshold of announcing that you are a meaning maker and take an involuntary step backward. The mantle of meaning maker is there for you to don, but you're likely to shake your head and refuse.

Let me try to meet your possible objections one by one.

Your first objection may be that donning the mantle of meaning maker is somehow an arrogant, pompous, self-important thing to do. At the heart of this objection is a misunderstanding of the difference between standing up for your own cherished beliefs and principles, which you know is not arrogant, and squashing other people underfoot, a position you are right to condemn. "I am living by my principles" is not identical to "You do not count." Does it feel arrogant to say, "I am living by my principles"? No. I think it feels grounded, sincere, and honorable.

A second objection may be that to self-nominate and don the mantle of meaning maker is to break with tradition. Most traditions wag a finger at anyone who announces that he knows what he knows and believes what he believes. You must indeed break with any tradition that demands that sort of obedience from you. Even in a tradition like Zen Buddhism, where a central tenet is that no one should claim more knowledge than anyone else, the very hierarchy that produces Zen masters supports the unspoken principle that some people are on top and others should defer to them. You will need to choose what part of your tradition you can accept — if any. Do not let the mere existence of a tradition stop you from donning the mantle of meaning maker.

A third objection may be that *making meaning* is an obscure and even unintelligible term. It's easy to throw up your hands and cry, "I don't get the idea of meaning-making. How can you make meaning? Either there is meaning or there isn't. No, I don't get it — so I think I'll pass!" This objection is both reasonable and disingenuous. It is disingenuous because we know perfectly well that *making meaning* is composed of ideas such as personal responsibility, courage, engagement, and authenticity. It is a far less mysterious term than those used by billions of people as pillars of their belief systems. Part of this objection, though, is not at all disingenuous. It is the part where we cry out in pain. What we are objecting to is not the obscurity of the phrase but the nature of the universe the phrase posits. *We object to a universe where meaning has to be made.* The way to meet this objection is with a certain maturity of being; we quietly demand of ourselves that we face up to reality.

A fourth objection may be that making meaning demands too much honesty and personal responsibility. How can you smoke two packs a day and also claim to be making meaning? How can you kick your dog as a stand-in for your boss and also claim to be making meaning? You can't — and you know it. As long as you prefer not to take responsibility for your life, you will sprint away from the idea of making meaning. However, most people would love to take responsibility and make themselves proud — they only fear that they know themselves too well. They have drifted off too many diets, squandered too many hours, and failed to rise to the occasion more times than they care to remember. If this is your history, you can leave it at that, remain disappointed in your efforts, and throw in the towel. Or you can take a deep breath, locate the place inside you that relishes effort and that takes pride in trying, and cast aside this objection.

A fifth objection, a cousin to the last one, may be that making meaning is just too much work. You want to kick back — you don't want to make meaning. You want to cross items off your to-do list and then be done with work — you don't want to make meaning after seven in the evening, on weekends, on holidays, and around the clock. Fair enough. But our lives are indeed the sort of epic projects that require work and attention. Try to accept that making meaning is indeed work, but then construe it as the loving work of self-creation. Meaning-making work isn't slave labor but rather a manifestation of the loving attitude we choose to adopt toward ourselves.

A sixth objection may be that making meaning involves too much choosing, which in turn produces too much anxiety. Choosing does produce anxiety; and constant choosing can produce constant anxiety. Most people will do almost anything but think too hard or too long about the choices confronting them. It is therefore natural that we might not want to make meaning, a process that amounts to making one reasoned, careful choice after another. But the more you avoid choosing and the more you impulsively or irrationally make the choices you can't avoid, the more trapped you become. Freedom equals constant, mindful choosing. Why not brave the anxiety that comes with frank and reasoned choosing and make yourself proud?

A seventh objection, related to the last one, may be that making meaning increases our core anxiety. Isn't one of our goals to reduce our experience of anxiety, not increase it? Well, maybe reducing anxiety isn't such a worthy goal. Our nervous systems say that this is irrational, but our hearts know it is appropriate. If we intend to hunt down a life-saving herb in a mosquito-infested jungle, we can't also hope to avoid anxiety. In order to accomplish our meaning-making tasks, we are obliged to say, "Okay, anxiety. Bring it on!"

An eighth objection may be that opting to make meaning guarantees that meaning will never be settled. How unsettling to be for a war one day and against it the next, or against it one day and for it the next, as our subjective sense of the war's meaning changes! We know in our bones that this is among the worst feelings possible, having our sense of the world turned upside down. We don't want this to happen, so we adopt simple positions, such as always being for or against the war our country is waging. But what you gain in safety you lose in righteousness. You can live a settled life but only at the cost of your authenticity and integrity.

You might raise other objections, and I could meet them all, but that would surely tax your patience. I think you understand the main point: that nominating yourself as the hero of your own story and deciding to lead a life devoted to intentional meaning-making comes with profound challenges — but so does any thoughtful, decent, righteous way of living. Will you make some choices and some meaning investments that you later regret? Of course. Will you feel unequal to making meaning on a given day? Of course. But opting to live this way, as the hero of your own story, brings the greatest rewards, among them a sense of dignity, real accomplishments, and the experience of joy.

CHAPTER 9

YOU DECIDE HOW TO MATTER

IT IS ONE THING TO DECIDE to make meaning. It is a quite
another to know *how to do that*.

What sort of enterprise are we talking about? Is it the attitude you adopt, maybe an ethical attitude roughly captured by
the phrase "I will try to do the next right thing and the next
right thing after that"? Is it some step-by-step process of rank-
ing competing pulls or weighing the value of an action? Is it
something like a knowing gesture — an existential shrug that
translates as "Let me just 'trust my intuition' and plow ahead"?
Could it be resorting to a single principle or homily selected
from all possible principles and homilies, maybe a version of
Kant's categorical imperative, the Christian Golden Rule, or the
new age "Do what you love"? What sort of thing are we looking
for: an attitude, a process, a scheme, a set of principles, a set of
tactics, a rule — what?

Let's consider one aspect of existence: making decisions.
How do you make decisions that help you feel as if you have
earned your experience of authenticity? How do you choose between competing pulls? How do you compare the values of actions? How do you make decisions when you can't predict their
consequences? What does embracing the existential ideal of
earned authenticity entail if you have to decide which road to

take with no idea where the roads lead? Ultimately, aren't you reduced to flipping a coin and admitting that life is an absurd crapshoot?

Indeed, don't we often act as if we are making up our minds and engaging in some rational process when in fact we've already made up our minds somewhere outside conscious awareness and for reasons we've never examined? Consider the following parable.

Jack puts his dad in a nursing home. Over a beer one evening his friend Bob asks him, "How did you happen to choose Cherry Pines for your dad?"

Jack replies, "I ripped out all of the pages in the phone book with nursing home listings, put them up on a wall, and threw a dart."

Bob's eyes open wide. "Really? Isn't that a little —"

"A little what?"

"I don't know. Unscientific? Immature?"

"Not at all! I trusted that my intuition would guide the dart."

"You're joking, right?"

"I am not. I also checked my horoscope. Throwing a dart seemed in line with my horoscope. It didn't exactly say, 'This is a good month to throw a dart,' but it did say, 'This is a good month to use the full powers of your intuition.' That was pretty clear."

"Jack," Bob exclaims, "I know you're pulling my leg. You didn't really throw a dart."

"I did."

"But — why? Didn't you have some good reasons to choose one home over another?"

"Ah, I had many good reasons. I also had many shadowy reasons. For instance, the home should be close to me so that I could visit dad a lot. But it should also be very far away from me, because I would like to put dad out of my mind and not be bothered with him. So how do you pick a place that is both very close to you and very far away? I thought about that for a few days, and it made my head hurt. Finally I decided that not having my head hurt was what was most important. That's when I came up with the dart idea."

"But —"

"No, seriously! This way, if I hit on one close to home, I would have to say that I was fated to see my cranky old dad a lot. If I hit on one far away I would be secretly thankful for the outcome, but no one could blame me. You'd have to blame the dart! So I gambled. In the first case I would have bitten the bullet and done 'my duty.' In the second case I would have gotten darned lucky."

"Which...where is Cherry Pines?"

"Three hundred miles away! I doubt I'll be able to see Dad very often!"

The two friends fall silent and sip their beers. Finally Bob asks, "That really works for you? You don't feel guilty?"

"It was the dart, Bob! I never meant the old man any harm. The dart decided." Jack smiles benignly.

After a long moment Bob shoots Jack a quizzical look. "There were listings for nursing homes three hundred miles away in our phone book? That's a little surprising."

"Did I say 'phone book'?" Jack replies, grinning from ear to ear. "I meant 'phone books.' I had to give the dart a fair chance, didn't I? I ripped out listings from phone books covering a three-state area!"

Jack is being honest. He wants his father at a distance, and that truth may not make him proud but that is his honest desire. Therefore he sets up his decision-making process in a certain way so that the outcome he wants is possible. He can even guarantee the outcome he wants if the only phone directory pages he throws his dart at come from out-of-state phone books. Isn't that what "throwing a dart" usually means: using some gimmick to second a decision we have already made? That can't really be the way to make meaning or earn the psychological experience of meaningfulness, can it?

If there is a better way to making meaning than throwing a dart that only confirms a decision secretly made earlier, what might it be? And if there is no good answer to this question, only haphazard, second-rate answers, might not that be the very truth that is leaving people breathless, sad, and at the mercy of their own shadows?

The answer can't be to exert willpower or to be disciplined. Neither willpower nor discipline will help you know whether you should go to medical school or pursue your dream of becoming a professional tennis player. Nor will a method suffice, such as listing all the pros and cons of every decision, because that still begs the question as to what criteria you would use to decide which list, the pro list or the con list, was the more compelling one. The thing we are looking for can't be a personality trait like discipline or a method like listing the pros and cons. Those fall short.

I've asked hundreds of people questions aimed at learning how they make their decisions when something important is at stake, such as in the following scenarios:

> It's important that I quit my day job and start a home business because I love the idea of being my own boss and because the flexibility of working from home will allow me to spend more time with my children. It's also important that I don't quit my day job because we need the financial security of a salary and because I doubt that I really have what it takes to create a successful home business.

It's important that I write my memoir because my story will help others and because I want to see my name in print. It is also important that I don't write my memoir so that the wrath of family members isn't visited on my head and so that I don't feel too vulnerable and exposed.

It's important that I confront my son about his drinking because he's driving dangerously and because he may be on his way to becoming an alcoholic. It's also important that I don't confront my son about his drinking because I know my son well enough to predict that my confronting him will lead to a complete rupture and will maybe ruin our relationship forever.

It's important that I devote at least fifty hours a week to my law practice, because if I don't I can't meet my obligations or advance at work. It's also important that I don't devote as much as fifty hours a week to my law practice, because working that much leaves me too little time for my family and for enjoying life.

I regularly ask people, "When two 'opposite' things matter to you, how do you choose which one you will pursue?" Here are four characteristic answers.

Natasha explained:

There was a time when my daughter was acting out self-destructively. The opposites I faced consisted of not speaking up or of speaking up, of maintaining the status quo and hoping for the best or confronting her and risking losing her to the streets. I chose by some felt sense and navigated the waters of our stormy relationship with a push here and a pullback there. I moved in the dark, as it were, steering by the guiding star of staying in relationship with her. I worked with whatever mental or physical behavior presented itself in the moment as having the potential for movement toward her greater good. Her health, her mental stability, and the safety of her physical being were my main concerns. I trusted and relied heavily on the sturdiness and strength of our vessel, our mother/daughter relationship, and chose by the seat of my pants.

Roberta wrote:

I'm embroiled in one such dilemma right now, and it involves a lot of agonizing about the risk in moving forward, despite my scary lack of foreseeable income. The move forward to a new painting studio situation will involve time, money, and the loss of a familiar and safe environment but will decrease my isolation and hopefully provide more opportunities for moving my artwork into the public eye. I made a huge list of all the advantages and disadvantages of staying put and of moving forward into this opportunity. There were many more reasons to stay put, if I looked just at quantity, but the reasons to move ahead seemed much more compelling, even though they were fewer in number. And my heart wanted to move forward. So I'm moving ahead. I think it is ultimately healthier to make the wrong choice for the right reason, and therefore I will move forward, albeit with trepidation.

Jonathan wrote:

Seven years ago I got divorced. At the time my sons were seven and two years old. During the time leading up to my divorce I struggled. I knew that divorce would completely alter their lives. I also knew that they would not see those changes as positive. I take pride in being a very involved, caring, connected father. I remember contemplating their reactions. I knew they would be hurt. Fathers are not supposed to inflict that kind of pain on their children. But I also knew that staying in that marriage would kill me. Healthy people are not supposed to subject themselves to such a relationship. In the end I chose divorce. But then I invested a lot of energy into making both the transition and the "new reality" for the children as painless and healthy as possible. This journey has led me into some dark alleys and dead ends but I firmly believe that I am a better person and father.

Anne wrote:

Having cancer when I was twenty-six had a huge impact on my life. Some things you just do. You drink the radioactive iodine! You have the surgery! You just do it. Fear is unimportant; you just do what you have to do. With other things fear can get in the way of deciding. Then I have to ask myself, Why in the hell am I so scared of that? My parents needed a caregiver, and I stepped up to the plate. I couldn't let my fears matter, and walking away was not an option. I've just started riding horses again after forty years — even in this bad economy and even though I have bad knees, not riding is not an option. But when it comes to my performing — there fear stops me. I see the choices and I don't really choose, I just let the fear win. I need to get performing into that category of things that aren't options! But I don't think I can; I never have, not consistently.

It would be unfair to say that these people are not trying to matter. You can hear their effort, their intelligence, and their ethics. Natasha made her choices "by the seat of her pants." Roberta opted for what felt "compelling" and what "her heart needed." Jonathan opted to "save his life." Anne faced life as if fear were the primary enemy — but her "there is no option!" battle cry couldn't lick her fears about performing. Do they each deserve credit? Yes. Have they landed on anything resembling a method? No, not really.

Maybe there is none. It may behoove us to accept that. At the same time, something like a method or set of principles does flow from the existential ideal. It sounds like the following: You weigh your actions against a vision you have of the person you would like to be, the person it would make you proudest to be; you take action; you learn from your experience to what extent you guessed right; and you make use of what you've learned as you weigh your next decision. We can give this a shorthand name: the principle of personal pride. You use the principle of personal pride to make your meaning. This may be the beautiful, imperfect, harrowing way — the *way* of making meaning.

CHAPTER 10

YOU HONOR YOUR WANTS, NEEDS, AND VALUES

IN ORDER TO EARN A SENSE of personal pride, you must factor in your wants, your needs, and your values. This is a dynamic process that requires you to step back and sort through the conflicting demands that life and human nature place on your system. Your appetite pulls you in the direction of more peanuts, sex, and experience. Your ethical sense requires that you do the next right thing and not shirk the responsibilities of freedom. Part of you wants nothing more than to recline and watch the sunset and part of you wants to go on a great adventure. Part of you is hampered by an ever-present whiff of your mortality, and part of you feels that you, or something about you, will live forever. You step back from all this, honor its complexity and its contradictory nature, plot your life course, and make decisions.

The decisions you are obliged to make are enormous. If your only goal were to make money, win at the games you play, or march in lockstep with your culture, that would be one thing. But what if you need more meaning and purpose in your life than that? Then you have to become a master negotiator, allowing yourself your pleasures, factoring in survival, protecting your self-image, minimizing your shadows, and, above all, translating your values into a life-purpose vision that, like a gyroscope, keeps you on course.

Authenticity demands that value trump appetite — and even survival. We all want principled action from ourselves. We all want to feel proud when we look in the mirror. Usually we think of this as leading a life of value or a life based on values. But existential ethics makes a higher demand than that you opt to honor values. It demands that you see through the idea of value to the more complex reality of earned authenticity. Loving values and having values are not enough. *Contextualizing* values is a much more difficult affair.

Anything can be valued, both because human beings can find value in anything and because the very word covers a variety of usages. You can "value" a steak sandwich for its juiciness, a car for its reliability, or your battle with cancer for "what it teaches you." You can value apparently contradictory ways of being such as "disciplined" and "spontaneous." You can value apparently contradictory ideas such as "peace" and "self-defense." Loving values, honoring values, and having values are not the same thing as knowing what to do in a given situation. For that, something else is required.

Consider the following list of values. On it are values associated with the humanist tradition, the wisdom traditions, the human potential movement, and our shared sense of what it takes to live ethically, instrumentally, and well.

Values List

Abundance	Altruism
Acceptance	Animal rights
Activism	Anxiety relief
Adaptability	Appreciation
Adventure	Aspirations

Authenticity
Autonomy
Awareness
Beauty
Belonging
Calm
Care
Challenge
Change
Civil rights
Clarity
Collaboration
Comfort
Commitment
Communication skills
Community care
Compassion
Connection
Considerateness
Contemplation
Courage
Courtesy
Creative expression
Creative thinking
Curiosity
Democratic institutions
Detachment
Determination
Difficulty
Diligence
Discipline
Discovery
Diversity

Ease
Education
Emotional health
Emotional intelligence
Empathy
Empowerment
Encouragement
Energy
Engagement
Enterprise
Enthusiasm
Equality
Equanimity
Excellence
Existential intelligence
Experimentation
Expressiveness
Fairness
Faith
Faithfulness
Familial care
Financial security
Flexibility
Flow
Forgiveness
Freedom
Friendship
Generosity
Genuineness
Goodness
Grace
Gratitude
Growth

Happiness
Healthy living
Helpfulness
Honesty
Honor
Humanism
Human rights
Humility
Humor
Imagination
Independence
Initiative
Inner peace
Innovation
Inquiry
Inspiration
Integrity
Intimacy
Intimate relationships
Intuition
Inventiveness
Joy
Justice
Kindness
Knowledge
Labor
Laughter
Leadership
Learning
Legal rights
Leisure
Love
Love of challenge

Loyalty
Meaning
Moderation
Mutuality
Nature appreciation
Open-mindedness
Openness
Optimism
Originality
Passion
Patience
Peace
Persistence
Philanthropy
Physical health
Piety
Playfulness
Pleasure
Possibility
Privacy
Productivity
Purpose
Quality
Rationality
Receptivity
Reliability
Resilience
Respect
Reverence
Reverie
Risk aversion
Safety
Scientific method

Self-actualization
Self-control
Self-direction
Self-forgiveness
Self-knowledge
Self-protection
Self-reliance
Self-trust
Serenity
Service
Silence
Sincerity
Sociability
Social cooperation
Solidarity
Spirituality
Stewardship
Stoicism
Strength
Success

Survival
Temperance
Tenacity
Thoughtfulness
Tolerance
Toughness
Tranquility
Transcendence
Trust
Truth
Truthfulness
Understanding
Valor
Variety
Victory
Vision
Vitality
Wealth
Wholeness
Wisdom

These are lovely words, ideas, and ideals. And quite an exhausting list! You can see at a glance the problem with trying to honor or make sense of such a diverse, contradictory catalog. Let's take some pairs on this list, say, "human rights" and "humility," "meaning" and "moderation," or "trust" and "truthfulness." Won't humility get in the way of fighting for a human right? Won't moderation prevent you from working exhaustively for the sake of meaning? Can you trust someone whose idea of truthfulness is to tell you everything that is wrong with you at every opportunity he gets? Any pairing of values provides these sorts of conundrums.

You can't live a value-based life just by feeling allegiance to certain values. It is one thing to value compassion, discipline, freedom, and gratitude. But what will you do when the principal at the school where you teach censors your class materials? Feel gratitude that you still have your job or that your principal didn't do worse? Feel compassion for his concerns and the pressures on him to prevent free expression? Decide to just continue acting in a disciplined fashion as a teacher? Or fight for your freedom by speaking up or taking action? Any one of these decisions might be "value based" — but how different they are!

A list of values is ultimately perplexing. You will see on such a list values that you prize as well as values that you do not prize all that much but that someone else esteems highly, making it seem as if values perhaps come rank ordered in your being. You will see values that flow from one vision of the world — say, a belief in God and values such as piety and reverence — and values that flow from another vision of the world — say, a naturalistic view and values such as experimentation and the use of scientific methods. It is surely no straightforward matter knowing what to value!

A list of values like the preceding one can serve only as a starting point in your understanding of the relationship between values and authenticity. Try the following experiment. Look over the values list and sort those values that strike you as significant into the following two categories, "ultimate values" (values that are intrinsically significant to you — values that you would hold no matter what — say, perhaps, freedom) and "instrumental values" (values that you only hold in order to accomplish your goals — say, perhaps, discipline). If you find it sensible to sort values into these two categories, what does it suggest about life as it is lived that some values feel ultimate and others feel only instrumental?

Or try this experiment. Choose any value from the list that you consider important and explain how it actually functions in your life. Say that you value "love." How do you love? Who do you love? How often do you love? Do you love everyone on principle, or do you only love those people who deserve to be loved or who earn your love or who engender a loving feeling in you? Pick one value and discuss with yourself what that value really means to you, how it actually operates in your life, and what it might mean to optimize that value.

Or try this one. Cross out all the values on the list that you think you should prize but that you don't actually care about. Once you complete this task, check in with yourself about how it felt to cross those values off. Isn't it odd and disturbing to realize that we might prize certain values not because we actually care about them but because we believe we should? Imagine spending your life upholding a value that you never really honored! Or, alternatively, imagine pestering yourself your whole life long because you aren't honoring some value that you don't give a fig about but only believe you should be honoring!

Or try this experiment. Pick a value on the list that strikes you as unimpeachable, and ask yourself the following question: "Is this a value that is significant to me because I would like to see everyone manifesting and championing it?" Might you honor a value not because you actually want to but because you feel it would be a good thing if all people valued it? Are some values not precisely yours — you could see yourself easily ignoring them — but rather part of a vision you hold for what would make for a good world?

Or try this one. Pick a value from the list that you find significant. Can you picture a set of circumstances — say, in wartime, if your family were threatened, if you moved to a different culture, or if you only had a short time to live — in which you would no longer prize that value? If you can picture such a set of circumstances, what does that imply about the permanence or impermanence of values?

Or try this last one. Choose ten values that you find worthy. Could you live in such a way that these ten values are present in your life every day? Could you even be expected to keep track of ten values as you go about your life? Is three or four a more reasonable number? Or might you be able to track a great many of them if you had some mental system that held them close?

Having tried these experiments, you will see that living a value-based life is not the same thing as drawing up a beautiful list of values. Nor is it the same thing as drawing up a list of principles like "Don't kill" or "Don't lie" — even if the list included our own first principle, "Make yourself proud." The same problems occur with that sort of list. In addition, even if it were possible to choose some values or adopt some principles in a static and everlasting way, what would happen to our wants and needs? Would our values or principles always trump our wants and our needs, or would they only trump them some of the time? If the latter, when would the trumping be justified?

One sort of answer to the dilemma of "what to do with a list of values" is the following: you coordinate your wants, needs, and values by holding to a life-purpose vision. That vision, arising from the conclusions you draw about life, becomes a reminder that every want, need, and value is up for grabs and can only be embraced or rejected according to whether or not it supports the ideal you've created for yourself.

CHAPTER 11

YOU CREATE A LIFE-PURPOSE VISION

IT IS BOTH IMPOSSIBLY HARD and absurdly easy to create the personal ideal mentioned in the preceding chapter. It is as easy as saying, "I want to be the best me possible" or "I intend to make myself proud," and meaning it. It is also impossibly hard, because it involves connecting the dots among your desires, your appetites, your dreams, your goals, your values, your principles, and everything else pressing down on you and welling up within you. If you were to try to connect all those dots, by, for example, creating a document as long as a manual by which to live, you would likely never dip into that manual or make any real use of it. The better answer — and a really good one — is to keep it simple.

You might start by creating a life-purpose sentence or statement. In one great gulp you take into account the values you want to uphold, the dreams and goals you have for yourself, and the vision you have for comporting yourself in the world, and then you spend whatever time it takes turning that unwieldy, contradictory material into a coherent statement that reflects your core sentiments about your life. You might, as a result of your efforts, come up with something like the following, a sentence that I first introduced in my book *Coaching the Artist Within*: "I will make use of myself every day in the service of truth telling while at the same time getting some real satisfaction out of life through love and work." This is an example of a life-purpose statement that, while hardly including every guiding idea of importance, is rich enough to serve.

Here is the life-purpose statement that Joan, a painter, created and sent to me: "I will triumph over the evil that was done to me, which gave me false limitations. I will participate in loving relationships. I will live well and make a meaningful life by working hard to become the best painter I can be, through drawing and painting five or six days a week." Marcia, a singer-songwriter, trying to manage her mood swings and her stress, riffed on the word *instrument* in her statement: "My instrument is tuned for the world to move through me. I care for my instrument and keep it tuned. I take care about how I place my instrument in the world."

Here are eight more life-purpose statements, created by coaching clients of mine. Each is personal and idiosyncratic, just as yours would be.

Pamela: "Action and satisfaction, today and every day."

Sylvia: "I bring my complete self to each moment."

Frank: "I take pride in working with my hands and doing the right thing. I want to die while building a chair, in bed with my wife, or agitating for some cause."

Sonia: "I am at ease in the universe as long as I speak in my voice, appreciate life, and work hard at the things I love."

Lois: "Right here, right now, paying attention and making meaning."

Harrison: "Years of creating a body of work, days of grace and enthusiasm."

Judy: "Passion and presence, courage and conviction."

Barbara: "All contradictions are reconciled if I am for the good."

Your life-purpose statement might be a word long, a sentence long, or a paragraph long. A life-purpose statement any longer than that would probably prove unwieldy. Why not create your own right now? Work on it until you conclude that you have come as close as you can in mere words to capturing the essence of your many life purposes. You step back, scratch your head, smile a little at the nature of the task, and then in all seriousness try to grasp the essence of your life intentions in just a few words. Give it a try.

One of my coaching clients, Jessica, described her process of creating a life-purpose statement:

I created my life-purpose statement several years ago and I still use it today. Here it is: *To manifest the best that I can be: by honoring my wisdom and nurturing my body-mind-spirit; through hearing with inclusiveness and integrity; acting in creative and graceful ways; in order to relish the fun and joyful harmony of being. To make my life a playful celebration!*

It took me several months of work to sort out what I truly valued and wanted to focus on. I also constructed it in such a way that I could use the first and last sentences to form a brief powerful statement that I could easily remember and that encompassed the whole message in my mind. *To manifest the best that I can be* and *To make my life a playful celebration!* have become my meaning mantras.

The process of creating this statement really helped me explore not only the bigger things I value but also my daily activities. I was surprised by the true value I found in the small daily actions that I took for granted. Even doing something as simple as serving a meal prepared by the deli began to emerge as an opportunity to find deeper purpose in my life. Instead of thinking I was too busy to cook and would have to pick up something at the store to throw on the table, I began to see this as yet another opportunity to celebrate with play. "How can I present this meal that will make it really pleasant? Can I have some fun with this?" I don't mean that I started to get loopy by always planning a party. I just started to see my life purpose with the perspective that I wanted, as a playful celebration of life.

Matthew described creating his statement:
My efforts at creating a life-purpose statement took several attempts over a number of days. Nothing seemed right — and then it came to me very easily. I chose: *To live authentically at all times, to bring empathy and respect to all that I do, to the best of my capability every day. To allow my creative, intuitive self to flourish, to nourish, honor, and cherish my relationship with source every day. To never forget and always allow the freedom of laughter and silliness to weave through my days.*

I suspect that this is a work in progress, just as I am, and will change as I move forward. I feel like I am taking a vow. I guess I am, a vow to myself. I feel like I just married myself! Congratulations, me! I know that a life-purpose statement of this sort isn't an absolute but just a reminder or guide of the deeper self that I want to see keep emerging. But I need that reminder. Who doesn't?

Alexander wrote:
I had no idea what I was supposed to be doing and balked at the task — and maybe resented it. But the main thing was, I found it intellectually shoddy. Create a single sentence (or even a paragraph) to encapsulate a life? Come

on, now! But something about the exercise kept tugging at me. What actually resonated for me was the following odd thought: that sometimes I read a quote from someone and get the sense that everything I need is embedded in that quote — that the quote could be lived and followed. Well, if someone else's words could have that sort of effect on me, why not my own?

So I played with the exercise with a seriousness — maybe, a self-respect — that I don't usually muster. Finally I came up with *I own myself.* I think I had something in mind like possessing an owner's manual for the self — that there was a way to know what to do with myself in every situation if only I reminded myself that it was my responsibility to try. I'm sure that *I own myself* wouldn't work for most people, what with the word *ownership* being fraught with so much baggage. But I like it — and I respect it. Does it still stick in my throat to think that I have a life-purpose statement? Yes. Do I find it valuable nevertheless? Yes, I do.

Lisa explained:

Keeping it simple was the most difficult part of doing this exercise. I tend to write a lot of words and to not want to leave out anything that feels important. Although lots of details and specifics came to mind, I opted to stay with the essence of what my life is about. I came up with this: *I am on this earth living this life as the heroine of my own journey. I choose to live in a way that supports my values, my authentic self, and my highest potential. I can do this, and I feel good about the path I am on!*

My statement could probably be shorter, but for now I like it. To me it sounds real, and when I say it I feel like I have my feet on the ground and my purpose in place. It's an anchor for me and I need an anchor, since I can tend to start floating into space at times. What I like about creating a life-purpose statement is that by putting it down in words you create something tangible. It is there to mold, adapt and share. It becomes a magical talisman — a powerful, magical experience. At least, that's what it's been for me.

Once you've created your life-purpose statement you might want to do the following: translate those words into a feeling in your body and a message in your brain so that your life-purpose intentions become readily available to you. You want your intentions available all the time and in real time. How do you accomplish this translating? In a way it is a task like memorization, so repeating your life-purpose statement over and over is a start. Or, to be whimsical about it, you might hang it as a banner over the stage where your thoughts play themselves out.

How do you employ your life-purpose vision? Imagine that you have a life-altering decision to make about your future. Maybe you're toying with the idea of becoming a stockbroker; maybe you think you might want to pursue screenwriting. You adduce reasons why it might be rewarding to follow this particular path and conclude that it seems like a good idea and a good fit. Without a life-purpose vision in place you might be done with your decision-making process. With it in place, however, you stop and measure your new desire against your core vision. If they happen not to match, you pass. Your intentions for your life as expressed by your life-purpose vision trump your reasons for choosing this particular path.

What does this measuring look like? How do you set your desire to become a stockbroker or a screenwriter down beside a phrase like "I bring my complete self to each moment" or "All contradictions are reconciled if I am for the good" and measure one against the other? You don't. The phrase is not like a ruler. It functions more like an existential chime. It alerts you to the fact that whatever you are about to do — take a screenwriting class, order a Scotch, needle your brother, gamble for an hour — is an act in the project of your life that must be judged not only by ordinary standards but also by the standard of earned authenticity.

Because its central function is as an existential chime, your life-purpose statement could just as well be a wordless tone, an inner light, a single word, a way of standing, a certain smile — it could be anything that reminds you that you have a personal ideal. No doubt people would find it strange if before each decision you made — say, whether or not to wait for the light to change before crossing the street — you hummed a middle C or smiled a certain smile. But you might find it smart and important.

However, there is value in your existential chime consisting of words rather than a musical note or a smile. We conjure with words. Words have personal resonances. When, for example, we choose as our life-purpose statement "good works and staunch rebellion," we've created an existential chime but we've also created a microblueprint for living and an existential day planner. We know to be on the lookout for good works to accomplish and wrongs to right. Without these particular words etched in our brains, we might notice Big Doctor's illegitimate antics but not make an effort to speak out. With them in place, we hear about the creation of a new "mental disorder," our existential chime goes off, and we know to protest.

You may do an excellent job of identifying your meaning needs and make every effort to construct a life that matches your life-purpose vision and still end up in an imperfect situation in which meaning hangs by a thread. Yet that is success! Yes, it would be a greater success if your efforts produced the exact results that you craved. But too much in life is out of your control for that to happen routinely, even if our steady diet of movies with happy endings blinds us to that existential reality. Life is not a romance. You create your life-purpose vision, and then you do the best you can.

When we do math, we expect answers such as "4." When we construct the meaning of our lives, we come up with answers that sound more like, "I intend to write my poetry, even though it will never pay; to live in love, even though I am only mediocre relationship material (work on that); to raise children in love, even though I am scared to death that my critical nature will harm them (work on that); and continue with my day job, which I do not love, by finding ways to invest new meaning in it so that I feel like I'm not wasting my time — while simultaneously detaching from it, so that I'm not burdened by its residue when I come home wanting to write poetry and live the rest of my life." This sounds nothing like "4"! However, it is smart, self-aware, and admirable.

Your life-purpose vision is the inner template by which you measure life, and it remains that measure until you revise it. For revise it you may. A life-purpose vision is not a substitute for continually practicing self-awareness and monitoring the meaning issues in your life. When you agree to commit to making meaning you agree to participate in a lifetime adventure. As you live you gain new information about what you intend to value and what you want your life to mean. This new information matters; if you are using words to keep track, rather than a musical note or a certain smile, you will want to make sure that those words still fit. Even your musical note or smile might need to change!

How do you know if you've created the right life-purpose statement? You don't. There is no sure way to know. You create it; you live it; and then you see. People balk at doing what might actually serve them because they want a guarantee first. Try to break that habit. Create your life-purpose statement, or choose some other device that will work as your personal existential chime. Then employ it. Do you find the tinkling of wind chimes beautiful or annoying? Whether you find your own existential chime beautiful or annoying, listen to it. It announces, "Make yourself proud."

TO CONSTRUCT MEANING

CHAPTER 12

YOU USE YOUR EXISTENTIAL INTELLIGENCE

My existential intelligence is Soaking - day by day minute by minute The BIG WHY ... create

YOU ARE ABLE TO CREATE your life-purpose statement and engage in other meaning-making activities because you possess existential intelligence. Let's take a moment to trace the history of this concept before we update it and make it our own.

The phrase *existential intelligence* is a hazy construct that has arisen from the "multiple intelligences" conversation. In that context, it is likened to a taste for the big questions, a taste a philosopher, cosmologist, or cleric might be presumed to possess, and appears rather more like "taking an interest in" than like "being smart about." If, to take one example, you happen to pray a lot, you would earn a higher existential intelligence (EI) score.

When scales are constructed to measure EI, questions such as "Do you ever reflect on your purpose in life?" "Do you ever think about the human spirit and what happens to life after death?" and "Do you spend time in meditation, prayer, or reflecting on the mysteries of life?" are asked — and carry equal weight. Thus Jean-Paul Sartre, the father of existential philosophy; Frank, who fantasizes a lot about heaven; and Sally, who prays regularly, might all achieve an equally high EI score. That makes the construct more than a little alarming.

How did the phrase *existential intelligence* arise? For the past hundred years people were thought of — and thought of themselves — as falling somewhere along a continuum of intelligence that ran from high to above-average to average to below-average. It was never clear how much intelligence any of these stops along the continuum represented, so it was quite impossible to say whether a person of average intelligence had "enough" intelligence for a particular task, whether that task was learning theoretical physics or voting in an election. It was simply taken for granted that average intelligence — the intelligence manifested by most people — was enough to handle the ordinary tasks of living. And if it wasn't — well, what was the individual, society, or our species to do about it?

It was presumed that ordinary intelligence was intelligence enough to work in the world, abide by society's laws, and understand everything from contracts to the math lessons encountered in school. It was easy enough to suppose that a person who needed five cracks at the bar exam was not quite as sharp as a person who aced it on the first try and that a good checkers player was not quite the intellectual equal of a chess grandmaster. But distinctions of this sort remained impressionistic, arbitrary, and whimsical. Little was known or could be said about intelligence because the concept was murky at best.

Since so much about the concept of intelligence remained unexamined and unclear, it became increasingly easy to argue that intelligence tests did little more than measure whatever the creator of the test happened to be in the mood to measure. Such tests apparently told us very little about "real intelligence," "raw intelligence," or "natural intelligence." Since no other instruments were available to measure real, raw, or natural intelligence, a new way of looking at intelligence was bound to emerge. Therefore it came as no surprise that we began to hear about a new fish in the sea: multiple intelligences.

Howard Gardner, the originator of this way of conceptualizing intelligence, argued that people possess not a single unitary intelligence but several distinct intelligences. He named seven: linguistic intelligence ("word smart, as in a poet"); logical-mathematical intelligence ("number/reasoning smart, as in a scientist"); spatial intelligence ("picture smart, as in a sculptor or airplane pilot"); bodily kinesthetic intelligence ("body smart, as in an athlete or dancer"); musical intelligence ("music smart, as in a composer"); interpersonal intelligence ("people smart, as in a salesperson or teacher"); and intrapersonal intelligence ("self-smart, exhibited by individuals with accurate views of themselves"). Later he added an eighth: naturalist intelligence ("nature smart, as in a naturalist").

Because his scheme served many agendas, it caught on quickly. When Daniel Goleman proposed another type of intelligence, emotional intelligence, it likewise found a large, sympathetic audience. Anyone good at describing his emotions but bad at chemistry could now think of himself as "just as intelligent" as that boy in high school chemistry class who memorized the periodic table at a glance. Who wouldn't embrace the idea that whatever you happened to be good at made you something of a genius?

We were still left, however, with a large hole in the middle of the intelligence discussion. Even a moment's thought forced one to realize just how many disparate ideas were being squashed together into the intelligence package: natural differences, cultural differences, experiential differences, attitudinal differences, motivational differences, and so on. Most important to an existentialist, every formulation of intelligence, whether intelligence was conceived as unitary or as multiple, failed to address the following core question: What intelligence or aspect of intelligence allowed you to comprehend what anything *meant*?

Gardner nodded in the direction of this question by wondering aloud about the possible existence of existential intelligence. Then he sidestepped the matter. Branton Shearer, in a paper supporting his efforts to measure existential intelligence, described Gardner's sidestepping as follows: "Existential intelligence (EI) was proposed by Howard Gardner (1999) as a possible ninth intelligence in his book, *Intelligence Reframed*.... Gardner concludes that scientific evidence does not support its inclusion as one of the multiple intelligences (MI) because it fails to sufficiently meet several essential criteria. The two criteria that it fails to fully satisfy according to Gardner are cerebral specification and clearly defined cognitive components."

If you really do possess something that can be called "existential intelligence" — and I believe you do — then you will not want to wait until it is "located somewhere in the brain" and "clearly defined" before you make use of it. Let's take the bull by the horns and define it as follows: existential intelligence is that part of our natural inheritance that concerns itself with what things mean. It is the part that steps back, dons a wide-angle lens, and appraises in the realm of meaning.

EI is actually the *first*, or *primary*, intelligence because it and only it allows us to know what to do with our other intelligences. It may be the case that it is more proper to think of it as "intelligence aimed at existential matters" rather than as a special or separate kind of intelligence, but for the sake of our discussion let's adopt the nicely resonant phrase *existential intelligence* to stand for that part of us that concerns itself with *what matters*.

We may be capable in any number of ways, but we are just a bundle of capabilities until we apply our existential intelligence. Existential intelligence is the coordinating intelligence, *the* intelligence that all the other intelligences serve. You may be smart enough to build a very big bomb, a rocket to Mars, a cloning machine, or a two-hundred-story tower, but if you do not ask yourself whether you *should* build it, you have applied only your raw intelligence to the task and not your existential intelligence.

In the Gardner model, existential intelligence is construed as the capacity for conceptualizing deeper or larger questions about human existence, such as the meaning of life, why we are born, why we die, what is consciousness, and how we got here. It is perhaps all of that, but it is also a great deal more. It is the intelligence we use to appraise the meaning of our lives minute by minute. It is our existential intelligence that permits us to think through whether we should fight in a war or protest that war or whether we should embrace our culture or rebel against it. If we want to live authentically, then we are required to employ our existential intelligence.

None of the other intelligences help us know how we should construct the meaning in our lives. That we are fluent with words, fit for the Royal Ballet, or able to out-sketch Picasso doesn't help us know what we should *do* with that capability — or why we should use it at all. Existential intelligence is the only human faculty that permits a person to think in the domain of meaning and actively construct meaning. Even if EI is only a metaphor and a weak construct, what it stands for is a clear truth: that to a greater or lesser extent we have the ability to step back and reason our way through questions of meaning.

If you happen to be among those who possess high existential intelligence, there will be no way for you to dodge "the meaning thing." It will be on your mind all the time. You will see right through your own escape-and-evasion attempts and realize that you are compelled to interrogate yourself about meaning because you need answers. Your high existential intelligence will prove a demanding, driving, and pestering intelligence. It might be nice to surgically remove it — but how would you do that? By "going stupid"? No — you will have to live with it, and you will have to deal with it.

Consider the following rough analogy. If you have ordinary or average hearing, sound might not be much of an issue for you. If someone spoke to you too softly, that would constitute something of a problem; and on some days you might experience sound overload and need a vacation from sound. But on your list of personal issues, hearing would surely not appear. Furthermore, wouldn't you chuckle a bit at, feel superior to, and not really understand people who complained of sound being a tremendous problem for them?

But what if you had supersensitive hearing? Yes, it might prove a plus to be able to hear conversations across the room and a plus for your family, clan, or society that you had this power. But wouldn't that sensitivity to the sound of garbage trucks rumbling by and bees buzzing make life that much more difficult? Wouldn't you *really* need vacations from sound, because so much of your day would be spent dealing with it? You might make a tremendous spy and become a national hero — but how often during the day would you find yourself wincing?

It may well be the case that people with average existential intelligence and those with high existential intelligence live in different universes, just as a person with ordinary hearing and a person with supersensitive hearing do. It might be that average existential intelligence puts you in one relationship to the experience of meaning and high existential intelligence puts you in another, more problematic relationship. Maybe average existential intelligence allows you to more satisfactorily "settle meaning down," and high existential intelligence allows for no such solution or respite. All this seems possible.

It also follows that while you may not find it personally fortunate that you have a good bit of existential intelligence, since your high EI will continually pester you, it *is* fortunate for the species. Conscience arises from your existential intelligence, as do all the institutions that spring from conscience. Your existential intelligence helps keep civilization civil, enlightened, and humane. To you it may always remain a pest — but that pestering may serve the function of preventing our species from regressing toward the mean of barbarism.

Be that as it may, if you've got it, you've got it. Whether it amounts to a guiding force and a social good or a terrible pest and personal problem depends on the relationship you craft with it. If you enter into smart dialogue with yourself about the necessity of making meaning, if you think through how you intend to handle meaning crises, if you articulate what existential joy might feel like and what you might do to acquire it, then you will be *using* your existential intelligence to help you live authentically rather than just being pestered by it.

If you forget that you can be smart, you are likely to be stupid. Bobby Fischer famously remarked after blundering into a loss against Boris Spassky in their world championship chess match, "It's one thing to be a great chess player and another thing to play great chess." It is one thing to possess sufficient existential intelligence to make sense of meaning, and another thing to sit yourself down and use your faculties. We don't know why we have this ability, and we don't know how to talk about it properly. Nevertheless, it is there to be used.

Someone high in linguistic intelligence is not yet a poet. To become a poet she must actually write, revise, and try. She must decisively show up *as a poet*. You employ your existential intelligence in exactly the same way, by decisively showing up *as an existentialist*, as someone who identifies herself as a specialist in the realm of meaning.

CHAPTER 13

YOU FOCUS ON MEANING RATHER THAN MOOD

WHAT CAN PREVENT US from using our existential intelligence, making meaning, and living authentically? Our moods. The problem is not only that we may *be* in a bad mood — it is also that we have gotten into the unfortunate habit of constantly checking in with ourselves to see what mood we're in. Am I down? Am I very down? Am I down again? Am I down *because* I'm down? Hamlet pestered himself with the question, "To be or not to be?" and rendered himself limp and indecisive. We pester ourselves with the question, "Am I depressed or am I not depressed?" and fail to realize that this very checking in on our mood is a choice — and an unnecessary and unfortunate one.

What sort of answer would you expect if you checked in on your mood at a moment when you weren't actively making meaning? Naturally you would be down, since you are checking in with yourself at precisely the wrong moment! You work for an hour on your novel and write a lovely scene. Do you check in on your mood as you're writing? No. You've been making meaning and feeling fine and see no reason to make note of your mood. An hour later, suddenly resistant to writing and uncertain about your novel's direction, you sit brooding on your sofa and *then* you decide to check in on your mood. Surprise,

surprise! You notice that you're unhappy. *Why check in at exactly that moment?*

It is one of the universe's ironic little jokes that human beings check in with themselves about their mood at exactly the moment when their mood might be at its lowest. Rarely do we check in on our mood when we are having a good time or working hard on something engrossing. At those moments it goes without saying how we are feeling — just fine — and so we don't bother to announce our good mood to ourselves. We wait until we aren't occupied and aren't actively making meaning to check in. How brilliant is that?

Remember that mood is what we are referring to when we talk about "depression." The word *mood* only means a state of mind or emotion. But somehow it has been twisted into meaning a state of mind or emotion existing along a happiness-unhappiness continuum. The word as commonly used implies that we are always to some degree happy or unhappy and that we should be monitoring those degrees so that we know when our mood is "disturbed." But are human beings really always happy or unhappy? Aren't we often in no particular mood — that is, in a kind of neutral mood? Not only do we take the temperature of our mood far too often — we have created a monster out of the word.

Our current construction of the word *mood* gives unhappiness more of a central position in our lives than it ought to command. Unhappiness is a reality, but mood is a construct — and a tyrant. Is there really some continuum, with euphoria on one end and grief on the other, on which we can always find ourselves? Isn't it more the case that for large portions of our days and our lives we are in "mood neutral" and feeling perfectly fine in that gear? Isn't it highly artificial and unhelpful to check in with ourselves to see how happy or unhappy we are when we may not be in any particular state of mind or experiencing any particular emotion?

This is no small point. If you think that you are supposed to be "in a good mood" and you check in with yourself and don't find yourself happy, you are likely to think that you're unhappy. But what if you were under no obligation to be in any kind of mood all the time? What if it were perfectly acceptable to be in mood neutral? When you recognize these two important truths — that you can pay less attention to your moods and more attention to your intentions and that experiencing no mood or a neutral mood is perfectly acceptable — you rid yourself of a mind-set that keeps you primed for unhappiness.

This is another area where a culture-wide shift in language would alter our experience of reality for the better. Instead of having to be in a "good mood" or a "bad mood" we could be in a "perfectly satisfactory neutral mood." We could watch a ball game, answer emails, stand in line, and not pester ourselves about our mood. We could talk ourselves down from opting for unhappiness when we find ourselves in snarled traffic by reminding ourselves that a neutral mood is probably our best bet. We could actually live in the now and be present by focusing on our current meaning opportunities rather than on our mood fluctuations.

If we take our pulse too often what we come up against is our experience of the void. Remember where we have arrived as a species. For thousands of years we suffered from one sort of unhappiness as we lived at the mercy of storms, tigers, germs, and tyrants. Then, starting in the seventeenth century, we experienced four hundred years of the celebration — and inflation — of the individual. Certain amazing ideas bloomed, and some even more amazing realities followed. We got individual rights. We got the rise of science and technology. We got the sense that human beings might get to know themselves and their world through the application of self-awareness and scientific method.

We got progress on all fronts. A wild, strange euphoria arose: we mattered!

But disaster was brewing.

Existential writers as far back as the pre-Socratic Greeks warned that the better we got to know our situation, the closer we would come to psychological disaster. We would, by pushing back the curtain and looking reality in the eye, stand face-to-face with a reality so cold that the space between the stars would seem warm by comparison. We would get nothing from science except what science could provide; we would get nothing from civil society except what civil society could provide; we would get nothing from the truth except hard truth. We kept losing hope as each mighty idea came up against its startling limitations.

The more we announced that we mattered, the more we saw that we didn't. The better we understood that the dinosaurs could be extinguished in the blink of an eye by a meteor strike or some other natural disaster, the better we understood that we could suffer a similar fate. The better we understood the power of microbes, and even as we worked hard to fight them, the better we understood that something functionally invisible and endlessly prevalent could end our journey on any given afternoon. The more science taught us, the more we shrank in size — and shrank back in horror. You could build the largest particle accelerator the world had ever seen and re-create the big bang, and psychologically speaking you would end up with only more of nothing — *even* more of nothing, if that were possible.

Certain enormous twentieth-century events cemented this psychological disaster. Hundreds of millions of human beings already had been slaughtered before the Nazis' efforts at extermination, but never before had images of towering piles of bones appeared in darkened movie theaters as newsreel footage. Never before Hiroshima could our species picture with such spectacular clarity the possibility, verging on something like a certainty, that our species could vanish — even in our own lifetimes. Hiroshima and the Holocaust shattered our belief that we were an indispensable species.

It is this apprehension of cosmic indifference that we are forced to stare at when we check our moods in moments when we aren't actively making meaning. We had wagered that well-stocked supermarkets and guaranteed elections would do the trick and protect us from the void. They haven't. It turns out that this hundred-year-long *certainty* that we are throwaways has made life look completely unfunny. We can laugh together over a bottle of wine and make small talk about this and that, adding a kind of cultural laugh track to a very unfunny situation comedy. But in most private seconds there is no laughter. Rather there is a deep, wide, abiding "Why bother?" If we check in on our mood when we are thinking *that*, what else but unhappiness do we suppose we will feel?

We are at least lucky that our language doesn't allow for an infinite number of compound words, as does German or Inuit. The Inuits have so many words for snow because their language allows for compound words. The-snow-on-Bob's-roof becomes one word, and the-snow-I-hate-to-sweep-out-of-my-driveway becomes another. If English worked like Inuit, we would have millions upon millions of compound words for our sadness and our experience of emptiness. We would have compound words manufactured from feelings like the-sadness-I-feel-when-I-realize-it-is-Monday-again and the-emptiness-I-feel-when-I-remember-that-I-will-be-gone-in-another-decade-or-so. If we possessed a vocabulary like that, how nuanced and horrible would be our mood check-ins!

In this extended Age of Reason of ours, we chat with ourselves endlessly and pay close attention to what we are saying. Not only are we engaged in lifelong self-conversation, but we have gotten into the bad habit of taking each of our thoughts as gospel. We think, "Life stinks," and then believe that it does stink because we had that thought. But could it be the *thought* that stinks? Could it be that such a thought only supports our pessimism and our discontent and serves no good purpose?

Where is the voice that says, "How does that thought serve you?" You can take better charge of your mind and your life by not continually checking in on your moods, by not taking thoughts such as "Since I am not happy, I must be unhappy" at face value, by monitoring your self-conversations and keeping an eye peeled for the tricks you're inclined to play. If, during a vacation from meaning, you ask yourself "How do I feel?" what do you think you are going to say? Get smart not only about what you ask yourself but also about *when you ask it.*

Focus on your intentions, not on your mood. Do not zealously take the temperature of your mood as if that were a life requirement. Accept that a certain neutrality of mood is not bad but perfectly acceptable. Let go of the idea that "mood" is the measure of your well-being. It is far better to spend time in a neutral mood engaged in authentic work than to pester yourself about your happiness or unhappiness. Focus on meaning and not on mood, and you will reduce your experience of unhappiness.

CHAPTER 14

YOU SNAP OUT OF TRANCE

WE HAVE HYPNOTIZED OURSELVES into taking the temperature of our moods far too often. Thus, we operate from a trancelike state maintained by two powerful forces. The first is human defensiveness. We prefer not to see what is going on in our lives and defend ourselves against the reality of our situations by entering into a personal trance state. We sleepwalk through our job, hoping that we won't notice how much we dislike it. We dissociate from the abuse we're receiving. We sleepwalk through the chaos at home, praying that we can drown it out by turning up the music. We sleepwalk through our finances, avoiding the realization that we can't retire any time soon. We drift from day to day and year to year, half-asleep by design, convinced that an unlived life is less painful than reality.

The second force encouraging us toward trance is made up of the countless constituencies engaged in getting us to buy something. These seductive forces employ language and imagery to snare us in a cultural trance in which, too often with our cooperation, we are manipulated into nodding in agreement. We are pressed to buy the image of life that commercials promote; we are convinced that owning a home is bliss and that renting is un-American, that something that sells well is ipso facto good, that "free checking" comes without a cost, that a beautiful woman driving a car is proof of that car's reliability. Taken together, personal and cultural trance combine to lend modern life the feeling that we're just going through the motions.

What does snapping out of trance look like? Consider Jack, a man of forty. Jack finds himself very busy. He spends at least ten hours every day doing work of various sorts. At night he reads the newspaper and watches a little television before going to sleep. In his fantasy life he pictures himself as a professional skier or a professional poker player. He is very good at taking out the trash, paying his bills on time, and not noticing that he and his wife do not love each other, that, in fact, they can barely tolerate each other.

The rash that won't go away he attributes to stress. The sadness that dogs his steps he puts down to the state of the world. If you were to ask Jack what matters to him, he would almost certainly reply, "Oh, you know, my job, my wife, the kids, and a winning season for my team." Entranced, unable to see even as far as to the other side of his bed, where his angry, unfulfilled wife pretends to sleep, every morning Jack renews his pledge to sleepwalk through life.

To the question "How are you?" he always replies, "Okay." This "Okay" is actually a fantastically complex and condensed shorthand for his sense that he does not matter, coupled with his efforts at leading a proper and seemly life. His too-keen understanding of the void, his defensive attempts to ward off self-knowledge, and his belief in the necessity of conforming all echo in his rote and tepid "Okay."

One day Jack overhears his wife say to one of her friends, "Of course he thinks I love him. He doesn't have a clue." A knife enters his heart — but the pain is much duller than he might have expected. It's as if Jack has experienced the sharp pain at a prior time and is now only feeling something residual. He thinks that he ought to be devastated — but he almost smiles.

By that evening he finds the contents of his mind shifting. He isn't thinking about his home team; he isn't thinking about whether or not the trash needs taking out; he isn't thinking about the bills or problems at work. Instead he is thinking about an open door through which he might walk and of the unknown vista beyond. The next day, when someone at work asks him, "How are you?" he instantly replies "I'm excellent!" What he means is, "Enough of this trance! I am going to live! By golly, I believe I have been completely asleep. Now I am going to wake up!"

This parable is just that, a parable. We don't expect instant realizations and transformations of this sort to occur in real life. In real life it is very hard for Jack to wake up. His wife may run off with the butcher, and it is entirely likely that we will find Jack still going about his everyday business, going to work, taking out the trash, rooting for the home team, and noticing every so often that he is alone in bed. That is much more likely than a person suddenly waking up and deciding to live.

On the cultural level, we are pressured into trance every minute of every day. How hard it is not to salute a flag, not to applaud when others are applauding, or to see through the ruses concocted by people who spend their days calculating how they can manipulate us. Their focus groups help them create just the right message to sell us all-terrain vehicles that no one actually needs, designer clothes that do not fit real bodies, and video games that provide the visceral sensation of killing all one's enemies. The pride they take is not in their product but in their ability to manipulate their brothers and sisters.

As a result we get polished commercials, aimed at our primitive underbellies, that suggest that we are risking our children's lives if we don't purchase a vehicle able to ford raging creeks. We are peppered with words such as *best, new, improved,* and *famous.* We learn about a movie's opening-week gross, not its goodness; about some celebrity's latest stunt; and, most pertinent to our discussion, about some new disease, disorder, or problem — tired-elbow disease, small-eyelash syndrome — and about the drug that will cure it. It is awfully hard to fend off this torrent of beautifully crafted messages!

One seriously smarmy face among this veritable army of seducers is that of Big Doctor. Big Doctor is a contemporary cousin of Big Brother, the character and metaphor made famous by George Orwell in *1984*. Big Brother continues to watch you, and Big Doctor now treats you. His metaphors reign supreme. He is a grown-up, well-oiled version of his now-innocent-seeming ancestor, that dentist of the commercials: "Three out of four dentists recommend..." He is a salesman in a white coat describing the side effects of the antidepressant he is hawking in so sincere a voice that the side effects sound like benefits.

It is very hard for the average person to see through all this manipulation, especially because he has so many powerful reasons to collude with Big Doctor. He loves the promise that his sadness isn't sadness but something like a headache or indigestion. Even the smartest people are likely to exclaim, "This can't be sadness because it feels *too bad*. It must be depression." Better to reject a hard truth and make an appointment with Big Doctor. When it comes to human unhappiness, personal trance meets cultural trance, and the result is a booming industry.

We can't do much to stop the manipulators from trying to seduce us. But we can try not to volunteer. We can take a step back and cast a cold, hard look at what our culture is selling. We can refuse to swallow language just because it goes down easily. We can refuse to nod in agreement just because everyone else is nodding. We can remind ourselves that we are in the crosshairs, and that the manipulators' imperative is to hypnotize us, entrance us, and seduce us. They have so much to sell, and we are their customers!

The first step is the hardest: acknowledging how seductive it feels not to think too clearly about your motives. Imagine a fellow — we'll call him Bob — who hears about a popular Las Vegas show featuring a well-known hypnotist. This hypnotist can entrance anyone into parading around the stage like a duck. Bob's first reaction to hearing about that show is the crucial one: if he finds himself smiling, nodding, and ordering tickets, he is halfway to waddling. The hypnotist, the audience, the zeitgeist, the Las Vegas chamber of commerce, and the casino's publicist all contribute to the show's success. But ultimately it is Bob's eagerness that keeps the hypnotist in business.

For a show like that to be popular, Bob and his fellow human beings must volunteer. Do your best not to make your way up to that stage where the smiling hypnotist awaits. If others raise their hands, so be it. You can pass on that demeaning show and make meaning instead. If you aren't to sleepwalk through life, medicated and sad, you must rebel. Rebellion isn't just about overthrowing tyrannical regimes. It is also about overthrowing your own tendencies to volunteer for trance.

Coming out of Trance

CHAPTER 15

YOU RECKON WITH THE FACTS OF EXISTENCE

THE EXISTENTIAL IDEAL DEMANDS that you pay attention to the facts of existence — not as a judge might, as someone focused on whether existence is just or unjust, but as an engineer might, as someone devoted to the project of building a life. You pay attention to what constrains you and what affects you. You pay attention to the forces aligned against you and the ways your culture pressures you into conforming. You pay attention to what matters to you, whether that something is happening across the room, across the world, or in your own head.

You pay attention especially to those areas where you have decided to make meaning. If you intend to be an astronaut, you need to know if your eyesight is good enough. If you intend to be of service, you need to know the psychological consequences of serving. If you intend to live contentedly, you need to know how you'll address your occasional feelings of outrage. Astronauts are not permitted to wear contact lenses, serving just might make you feel servile, and anger at some injustice might rock your tranquility. Those are the sorts of facts that concern you because they pertain to your personal meaning-making efforts.

The task isn't identifying abstract facts of existence that seem most important — death, say, or the three facts of existence (impermanence, suffering, and insubstantiality) that Buddhists emphasize. Rather, it is reckoning with the concrete facts that impinge on your existence — the flood that washes away your home, the brain injury that removes a portion of your memory, or the opinions you hold that prevent you from experiencing enough meaning. The facts of existence include the inevitability of death and the reality of unhappiness, but they also include the everyday facticity of life as it pertains to you.

If you have noisy neighbors, that constitutes a fact of your existence. If you're bombarded by advertisements designed to sell you antidepressants to supplement your current antidepressant, that constitutes a fact of your existence. If you're caring for aged parents, that constitutes a fact of your existence. None of these facts may matter to someone else, but they indubitably matter to you. You do the brave thing, recognize where you are, and reckon with those real stresses and constraints.

When I was seven I contracted rheumatic fever. I lay in bed for some months with a paralyzed left leg. I would surely have died except for the kindness of a local doctor, who provided my mother, who was very poor, with medicine for free. During those months I couldn't make any meaning that required getting out of bed. If your left leg is paralyzed it is really and truly paralyzed, and it is a mental mistake to suppose that you can somehow avoid factoring that into your calculations about life.

When I was eighteen, the Vietnam War raged. That was a fact of my existence that could not be ignored. Every young man in America had to factor the Vietnam War into his calculations — and factor it in large. If you avoided registering for the draft, you became a criminal. If you registered for the draft and crossed your fingers, you had a good chance of ending up in Vietnam. I enlisted in the army. I didn't enlist for no particular reason. I enlisted because the Vietnam War was *the* fact of my existence at that moment. No male of my age could avoid reckoning with it, one way or another.

My son lives in the Amazon jungle. He built several boats for his fledgling eco-tourism business and rats ate them. Prospective European customers did not seem as interested in traveling down the Amazon as he had hoped, and building more boats (and protecting them better) seemed like the wrong course. So he aimed himself in the direction of a different meaning opportunity and now works with indigenous people to help them market their crafts. Every day scorpions the size of Maine lobsters cross his path. He and his family live in the jungle, a real place with monsoons, monkeys, and the encroaching forces of modernization and corporate globalism. Those are among the facts of his existence.

You can adopt a phlegmatic, philosophical, detached attitude as your way of moving through life, and that may serve you beautifully. However, the second you decide that you have an intention — say, to combat disease, write fiction, or protect freedom — your serene attitude will butt up against the world of contingent reality. It is fine to put a smile on your face or to be present at all times or in some other way to adopt a serviceable attitude, but if you have a certain intention — if you really intend to make meaning — then whatever prevents you from realizing that intention matters. Because it prevents you from realizing your intentions, it will bring pain and unhappiness — and *that* must be reckoned with.

We can only make meaning in the context of the real world. It is one thing — and an important thing — to get a grip on our minds. But it is a much more complicated thing to make meaning in a universe that is not set up to serve our meaning needs. Contingent beings like us can't make meaning separate from reality. It may be possible for us to completely take charge of our attitude, like an advanced monk or philosopher. But that isn't the same thing as making meaning. In order to make meaning we must threaten our equanimity by looking around and seeing clearly *what prevents us from making meaning.*

Some of the facts of our existence support our efforts at making meaning, and others stall our efforts. If you are condemned to hoisting stones until the end of time, you are free, like Sisyphus in Albert Camus's famous tale, to adopt a certain phlegmatic attitude vis-à-vis that condemnation. But you are not free to make yourself proud by painting a mural or building a school. Those options are not available to you if you are condemned to hoisting stones all day. You can only be free in ways that take that humbling lack of freedom into account — unless, of course, you manage to escape. If you are Sisyphus, you must escape or adapt.

The prime fact of your existence that you do have the power to escape is *who you have become*. You can't stop the reality of starvation; but you can stop stubbornly starving yourself. You can't stop wars; but you can stop your own road rage. You can't stop humanity from conjuring angels and devils; but you can personally grow up. If you have become someone who is too frightened of criticism to speak in her own voice, then you can't carry out your intention to write a revealing book until you reckon with that pertinent fact of your existence. You can't stop others from hiding, but you can stop yourself.

A coaching client of mine, a professor who'd edited many books but who until recently had never written one of his own, told me the following story when we began working together. He'd written a memoir. The first publisher he sent it to expressed a lot of interest and advised him that they would be pleased to publish it if he made a few changes. My client had perceived the changes as innocuous and expected that he could make them easily. But instead of replying, "Certainly!" he explained that he was very busy that semester and wasn't really sure when he could get to the editing.

Was he really that busy? No more than usual. Was he any busier than when he had written the memoir? No. Then why provide that odd response? Six months went by, and he hadn't begun the edit. The editor at the publishing house sent him friendly emails reaffirming her interest and wondering when she might expect to see the revised manuscript. He wasn't sure, he said; he remained very busy.

Another six months went by. Remarkably, the editor kept affirming her interest. The professor, for his part, kept replying that he was busy. He knew that he wasn't *that* busy. He knew that he would regret whatever it was that he was doing to kill his chances with this publisher. Still, he kept stalling. In everything else he claimed a wonderful rationality. He hated it that so many people, his students especially, didn't think and act rationally. So what was *he* doing? He could only shake his head. Finally he called me.

Even without knowing anything else about this professor's situation, anyone would find it easy to hazard some guesses. Maybe, since he had only edited books previously and had never written one in his own voice, he was worried about "coming out" in that voice and being laughed at. Maybe, since it was a memoir, he didn't want family secrets revealed, even though he claimed not to be worried about that. Maybe he was annoyed that the editor in question wanted *any* revisions — maybe some half-hidden grandiosity had activated false pride. Maybe he didn't actually know how to make the revisions and was fibbing when he claimed they would be easy.

Anyone might have come up with these hypotheses — but he had come up with none of them. He had never posed himself the question! This is the real Sisyphus, someone phlegmatically smiling at the enslavement that he himself has created. This professor had stubbornly refused to reckon with the facts of his own existence, with the fact that he'd become *such a person*. He had a lovely study, a lovely desk, a lovely view — and he was miserable, because his meaning intentions foundered on the shoals of his formed personality. But that reckoning had finally begun — calling me was the first step. As to the outcome: he never did complete that book, since it revealed too many family secrets, but he did manage to write and publish others.

How do you reckon with the facts of existence? The same way that you reckon with the fact that you have come to a river and are obliged to find a way to cross it. The river is real. Rarely will you find a sweet little rowboat sitting there on the bank waiting for you. You will have to do something — search along the bank for reeds to weave into a raft, spend a month or a year learning to swim, shouting until someone from the tribe inland hears your cries — something. If you stand looking at the river and waiting, you create unhappiness.

Say that you and your mate are not happy together. That is real. You have children together. That is real. You haven't worked outside the home in twenty years. That is real. Nor do you really want to. That is real. The economy is down. That is real. Your religion frowns on divorce. That is real. You will be poorer if you divorce. That is real. You know of innumerable women who have created successful lives after their divorce. That is real. You also know of many who haven't. That is real. This is the river on whose bank you stand. There is no bridge; there is no rowboat. There is only risk, and need, and the prison of your formed personality. And, yes, opportunity.

Existence is the mother of all cold showers. Whether it is frostbite in Siberia or malaria in the Sudan, a difficult childhood or a lonely adolescence, bills piling up or your self-esteem plummeting, you will have plenty of reality with which to reckon. This reckoning *is* heroism. It is how you earn your feeling of authenticity.

CHAPTER 16

YOU PERSONALIZE A VOCABULARY OF MEANING

IN ORDER TO LIVE A LIFE full of meaning you need to possess a vocabulary that permits you to communicate with yourself and others about the meaning realities of your life.

Without such a vocabulary, you can't identify what is actually going on in your life. If something disturbing is happening and you can't identify it as a meaning crisis, how will you handle it? You may misidentify it as a "depression" or a "work problem" or a "relationship issue" and head yourself in the wrong direction, toward antidepressants, a stimulant, a nap, or somewhere else that fails to serve you. If you possess the language to call it a meaning crisis, then you know what to do: you know to make new meaning, reinvest meaning, and so on.

Here are five phrases with which to start your personal vocabulary of meaning. Feel the shift in you as you speak these phrases, think about them, and take in what they represent.

Making meaning

"I make my meaning. I take responsibility for the meaning in my life, I arbitrate the meaning in my life, I take action in the service of the meanings I choose."

Meaning investment

"I make meaning investments. I decide each day where I am going to invest meaning and which parts of the day can be 'half-meaningless' without that bothering me. I understand that my meaning investments involve me in work and require that I act, but I recognize that only by making meaning investments can I live authentically."

Meaning opportunity

"I look for meaning opportunities. Meaning is not settled for all time, and as I change and as the world changes I keep my eyes open for new meaning opportunities. The many meaning opportunities available to me become my personal meaning menu, arsenal, or repertoire."

Meaning crisis

"I recognize meaning crises when they occur. If I'm feeling blue, if I feel a pull toward an addiction, if I begin looking for meaning substitutes, I know to stop everything and see if a meaning crisis has occurred. If it has, I know what to do next — use my meaning-repair strategies to make new meaning."

Meaning repair

"I am turning myself into an expert at meaning repair. I am learning exactly what to do to maintain and repair meaning when a meaning leak, lapse, or crisis occurs."

Sarah, a teacher, explained her take on meaning crises:
All my life I've struggled with meaning. I would look at others doing the things our culture considers normal and wonder how they could be meaningful to them. From there I would usually progress to wondering what

was wrong with me that these things held no meaning for me. Over and over I've struggled with bouts of depression arising from this misunderstanding. As I look back, I can see how these down times have been the result of meaning crises, not psychological problems — a label both I and others have used to identify what I was experiencing. Having a personal vocabulary of meaning is profoundly important. I feel like I can now guide myself through the undertaking of making meaning. With this vocabulary of meaning in place, I have a whole new understanding of life and my place in it.

How will you use your vocabulary of meaning? First of all, you use it in conversation with yourself. This might sound like the following:

Visiting my parents is a considerable meaning drain because my father still harps on how little money I'm earning from my music, and my mother can't get over the fact that I'm not married or interested in having children. Because it is such a meaning drain and almost always precipitates a meaning crisis that takes me months to get over, I am going to skip Thanksgiving this year. And I am going to skip it without feeling guilty, because avoiding meaning drains is crucial to my emotional health. At the same time, I'm going to make a new meaning investment in the CD I'm creating — both a new meaning investment and a financial investment — and exhaust myself in its service over the long Thanksgiving weekend. If I can make some meaning there and also avoid the meaning drain of going home, I will have created something like a perfect weekend, existentially speaking.

You also use your personal vocabulary of meaning when you speak to others, even if they don't share your vocabulary. This might sound like the following:

Hi, Mark, I wanted to tell you about the meaning adventure I embarked on last April. I had it in mind to make a little meaning by writing a song and singing for the May rally that I told you about. Just going would have been meaning enough; but I wanted to invest the march with a little additional meaning by writing a song that I've had in mind for months and then singing it to just the right audience. A meaning opportunity arose when that snowstorm hit and school was closed and I got two days off teaching. I invested those days with tons of meaning by getting up early every morning, dealing with my doubts about my songwriting skills and my singing talent, and sitting there at the keyboard actually writing the darn song! It was a real meaning effort and I ended up exhausting myself, so I had to sleep a lot the next day, but in the end I got the song written and got to sing it for ten thousand people, and it became one of the great meaning events of my life.

How do you acquire your personal vocabulary of meaning? By adopting the language I'm suggesting and/or by creating words and phrases that serve you. The process is simple, except that you will be hampered by self-consciousness. If no one else is saying, "You know, I invested yesterday with meaning by working on my novel from 6:00 a.m. until dinnertime," you may find it hard to say such a thing. If you can overcome your feelings of strangeness, awkwardness, and self-consciousness, just as you need to overcome them to speak any new language, the rest is easy — because your vocabulary will make perfect sense to you.

Build your vocabulary of meaning with words and phrases

that strike you as, yes, meaningful. You may prefer psychological language, spiritual language, existential language, or philosophical language. There are no words that work for everyone, not even the word *meaning*. All words are complex bundles of meanings, and a word that has a positive resonance for one person may have a negative one for someone else, or no resonance at all. Put words and phrases on the table as possible candidates for inclusion in your vocabulary of meaning and examine each one to see if it actually holds some meaning for you.

Following are some phrases that you may find useful to include in your vocabulary of meaning. Try each one out. Say it out loud. See how it sounds and feels. Try it out in conversation with yourself, and incorporate it into your vocabulary of meaning if it feels useful.

Action

"Making meaning requires that I take real, concrete action in the service of my meaning investments."

Authenticity

"When I represent myself in ways aligned with my values and manage to rise above my baser instincts, I feel as if I am living authentically."

Choice

"Since there is no path to follow but only paths for me to create, I know that I will be confronted by one choice after another — and the anxiety that accompanies choosing."

Context

"An activity that seems abundantly meaningful to me in one context may hold no meaning or interest for me in another context."

Contingency

"My ability to make meaning in my preferred ways is contingent on factors beyond my control, including whether the culture supports such efforts and whether I am physically equal to the challenge."

Engagement

"When I assert my freedom and stand up for my principles, I am involved in activism and am engaged with the realities of the world."

Existential anxiety

"Even when I'm happy, some existential anxiety continues to course through me, because I remain aware of life's fleeting nature."

Facts of existence

"A wise person takes the facts of existence into account when planning where to make his or her next meaning investment."

Freedom

"Many things are not in my control, but I have the freedom to decide how I will respond to life and where I will make my meaning investments."

Heroism

"I need to remember that heroism is required of me if I am to stand behind my meaning decisions and not let others dictate meaning to me."

Individuality

"Since I am the only arbiter of meaning in my life, individuality is a necessity."

Intentionality

"Many people move through their days passively, but I like to feel that I'm moving through my day with a strong intentionality."

Meaning accident

"My boss inviting me to take on the Jones account was a meaning accident that affected how I've made meaning for the past two years."

Meaning adventure

"When I started my first Internet business, it felt like the beginning of a great meaning adventure."

Meaning conflict

"Every time I start a novel I find myself embroiled in a meaning conflict, torn between believing that fiction is meaningful and believing that fiction is ridiculous."

Meaning container

"I hope that I'm doing the right thing by pouring meaning into anthropology. For now at least, anthropology feels like a meaning container capable of holding my beliefs and dreams."

Meaning distraction

"After spending the past six months working eighty-plus-hour weeks to launch my nonprofit, I needed a mindless meaning distraction. So I played computer solitaire for the entire weekend and didn't allow myself to feel an ounce of guilt."

Meaning divestment

"I'm making a meaning divestment from my career of the past ten years, career counseling. I don't want career counseling to lose all its meaning, but I need to make new meaning investments elsewhere."

Meaning drain

"I find my sister a real meaning drain. Every time I see her, she asks me why I refuse to get a normal career and what makes me think I'm so special."

Meaning duty

"After spending years refusing to take responsibility for my own happiness, I now know that the future I deserve is up to me. Accepting this challenge is a meaning duty to myself."

Meaning effort

"It's going to take quite a meaning effort to make my new research assistant job feel worthwhile. But I'm going to make that effort because I'm not ready to quit."

Meaning event

"I had a profound meaning event this morning when I realized that I do not need to find my father, who abandoned us when I was five."

Meaning goal

"I have as a meaning goal 'going organic.' This requires that I shop more carefully and be willing to spend more for the right foods."

Meaning invitation

"My meaning coach offered me a welcome meaning invitation when she wondered aloud if I felt ready to launch my home business."

Meaning lapse
"I was fully committed to my job, and then one day I heard myself say, 'Nobody really needs our product.' That meaning lapse caused me to second-guess everything about my life."

Meaning potential
"Many disciplines hold meaning potential for me, but I find it hard to choose one and stick with it."

Meaning problem
"I find biology intellectually interesting. But no amount of scientific knowledge can solve the meaning problems in my life."

Meaning repertoire
"I've built a large meaning repertoire of activities that are pretty much guaranteed to provide me with the experience of meaning."

Meaning shift
"I experienced a meaning shift from loving fiction and dismissing poetry to loving them both when I began reading the poetry of Rilke."

Meaning spark
"The Spanish movie I saw today was a meaning spark that caused me to rush home and resume work on my suite of paintings."

Meaning substitute
"I couldn't get to work on my dissertation so I settled for some meaning substitutes instead, first by reading the newspaper, then by reading a novel, then by watching an action movie."

Meaning support

"The books on my bookshelves are meaning supports for me. Their presence reminds me that I am not alone in caring about Greek philosophy."

Meaning task

"I've set myself the meaning task of better understanding the authoritarian personality."

Meaning vacation

"I took a meaning vacation this weekend and put aside all of my work. I had some frivolous fun and came back to my job on Monday completely refreshed."

Risk

"Since it is impossible to predict whether a given meaning investment will pan out and provide the experience of meaningfulness, each new investment is a risk that comes without guarantees."

When you use words like *depression*, you are pushed in one direction. When you use phrases such as *meaning adventure* and *meaning investment*, you set yourself off in a better direction. Whether you use my vocabulary, your vocabulary, or some combination of both, you owe it to yourself to speak in a language that supports your intentions.

CHAPTER 17

YOU INCANT MEANING

INTRODUCING A NEW VOCABULARY of meaning into your life is a tactic you employ to create fertile ground for meaning. Tactics of this sort are not to be scorned. Another tactic is the following one: using short breath-and-thought bundles called *incantations* to remind you throughout the day of your meaning intentions.

So many thoughts of all kinds pass through your mind on a given day that little space may be left for you to remember to invest meaning, grab a meaning opportunity, or handle an incipient meaning crisis. Incantations create that space. You produce a long, deep breath, and as you breathe you "drop" a thought into the breath. I describe this process in detail in my book *Ten Zen Seconds*.

In *Ten Zen Seconds* I described twelve all-purpose incantations that can be used to help you quickly center, among them "I am completely stopping," "I trust my resources," and "I feel supported." Each of the twelve incantations described in that book has a hidden existential component, which helps explain its power. For instance, "I am completely stopping" translates as "Even though I'm afraid that I may encounter a whiff of cosmic meaninglessness if I dare to stop completely, I nevertheless recognize that I must stop all my rushing if I hope to get centered."

I created the twelve all-purpose incantations in *Ten Zen Seconds* to be used in a wide variety of situations for centering and reducing stress. The following twelve new incantations are specifically designed to support you in your meaning-making efforts. I've divided them into two parenthetical phrases to indicate which part you say or think on the inhale and which part you say or think on the exhale.

1.   (Meaning is a) (wellspring).
2.   (I interpret) (the universe).
3.   (I nominate) (myself).
4.   (I invest meaning) (here). *now*
5.   (I accept) (the consequences).
6.   (I maneuver) (in circumstances).
7.   (I live) (with doubt).
8.   (I can handle) (meaning crises).
9.   (I'm in charge) (of my personality).
10.   (I limit my) (meaning vacations).
11.   (I relish) (meaning sparks).
12.   (I have energy) (and passion).

Let's look at each one in turn.

The incantation "Meaning is a wellspring" announces that there is a never-ending supply of meaning. For the nonbeliever, this never-ending source is the self. For the believer, this never-ending source is soul or spirit, a god or gods, Gaia or Universal Mind, or some other entity separate from the embodied self. However they arrive at their conclusions, both believers and nonbelievers can remind themselves of their conclusion that "meaning is a wellspring" by using this incantation.

"I interpret the universe" reminds us that meaning is subjective and that it is the individual and only the individual who arbitrates personal meaning. Each person must make independent, idiosyncratic sense of life and create her meaning intentions, in real time and despite the pressures put on her by her family, her peers, and her culture. As a contingent being she is too constrained to control her universe, but she is not prevented from interpreting it.

"I nominate myself" reminds us that our core existential task is donning the mantle of meaning maker. The meaning maker decides to make meaning and then nominates herself as the person who will make that meaning, as the one who leads, speaks, rebels, and does everything required to ratify her intentions. She nominates herself, elects herself, and serves — as the heroine of her own story.

"I invest meaning here" reminds us that life can be experienced as a seamless series of meaning investments that, even with the occasional meaning vacation factored in, produces the felt experience of steady purpose. The central strategy of a meaning maker is to announce her meaning intentions to herself, whether she is about to return emails at work or chat with her daughter. By consciously investing meaning *here* she imbues her life with a sense of personal meaning.

"I accept the consequences" reminds us that we have willingly agreed to accept the risks that come with commitment, engagement, and authenticity. We decide to matter — every day we recommit to and embrace that decision. Donning the mantle of meaning maker sometimes leads to predictable outcomes and sometimes to unpredictable ones, among them real-world setbacks and significant changes of heart and mind. "I accept the consequences" reminds us not to feign surprise when life throws us such curves.

"I maneuver in circumstances" reminds us that, if we are to meet our meaning needs and fulfill our meaning intentions, we must maneuver with cunning, courage, and effort in the minefield of reality. We are not free to sit back; nor are we free to make all the meaning we would love to make simply because our desire is strong. Our efforts are always contingent — on everything from the state of the world to the implacable pain of a sudden toothache. Circumstances arise; and we must maneuver.

"I live with doubt" reminds us that doubt is an inevitable part of the human experience and must be handled rather than dreaded. Meaning-making can be derailed if some particular doubt — for instance, about the wisdom of our paths, the morality of our jobs, or the viability of our intimate relationships — suddenly casts everything else in doubt, even including the availability of meaning. Incanting "I live with doubt" prevents us from turning any given doubt into a doubt about everything.

"I can handle meaning crises" reminds us that we are equal to dealing with the meaning leaks and meaning shifts that come our way (a plan for handling meaning crises is provided in an upcoming chapter). Among the tasks of a meaning maker are recognizing meaning crises as they occur, having strategies in place to meet them, and *believing* they can be weathered. Incanting "I can handle meaning crises" reinforces your belief that meaning crises, as horrible as they can feel and as difficult as they can be to solve, can never completely destroy meaning, since meaning is a renewable experience.

"I'm in charge of my personality" reminds us that not only must we look life in the eye — we must also bravely stare in the mirror. We can't make the meaning we intend to make if we allow the shadows of our personality to thwart our efforts. When we react defensively, sabotage ourselves, let our anger derail us, or in other ways defeat our meaning-making efforts, we disappoint ourselves and create the experience of meaninglessness. Incanting "I'm in charge of my personality" instantly returns the task of self-improvement to where it belongs — with you.

"I limit my meaning vacations" reminds us to monitor and

limit our breaks from meaning. It is fine if we take vacations from meaning by watching TV, shopping, surfing the Internet, playing video games, and so on — we do not need the psychological experience of meaningfulness twenty-four hours a day. But we need to remind ourselves that our vacations from meaning are not a *substitute* for meaning. Incanting "I limit my meaning vacations" both acknowledges the legitimacy of vacations from meaning and prevents those vacations from turning into crises.

"I relish meaning sparks" reminds us that meaning can be sparked — by a thought, decision, memory, object, anything. If you're a painter, meaning might be sparked by a trip to a museum. If you're a researcher, meaning might be sparked by a lecture you attend. It might be sparked by a photo in an album, a smile on your child's face, or the recollection of a meaning adventure. Incanting "I relish meaning sparks" is an invitation — for meaning to ignite right now.

"I have energy and passion" reminds us to draw on our energy reserves to meet our meaning needs and to approach our meaning investments with sufficient passion. Sometimes we have to tease out a little more energy and passion in order to feel proud of our efforts — if we stop short, we fail to experience the meaningfulness that is waiting just around the corner. Incanting "I have energy and passion" affirms that we have more inner resources than, in our tired or busy state, we may suspect we have.

How might you use these incantations? You can include them in your morning meaning practice, which I'll describe next; you can use them as quick reminders throughout your day of your meaning intentions. Use both the twelve all-purpose incantations from *Ten Zen Seconds* and these twelve meaning-oriented incantations to keep yourself centered and on course. As simple as they are, they serve as magical charms and can provide a physiological and psychological boost. Try them out — give them a chance to work their magic.

It is harder to be unhappy and harder to stay unhappy if, throughout your day, you say things to yourself such as, "Meaning is a wellspring," "I relish meaning sparks," and "I have energy and passion" — or similar phrases of your own creation. If you not only say such things but also stop rushing and breathe deeply, you will be making a singular commitment to your happiness. This is magic on a human scale: the magic of substituting language that supports your intentions for language that sinks you and makes you sad.

Your existential program is a matter of outlook and philosophy, but it is also a matter of tactics, strategies, and concrete actions. Adopting a personal vocabulary of meaning and incanting meaning are among the smart tactics you can employ as part of your existential game plan. So is the strategy we'll examine next: creating and maintaining a morning meaning practice.

CHAPTER 18

YOU MAINTAIN
A MORNING MEANING PRACTICE

IN ORDER TO STAY ON TOP of meaning and of knowing where you want to make your daily meaning investments, try instituting a morning meaning practice. It is best to reserve the morning for this practice, rather than penciling it in for some other time of the day, because making it a morning practice allows you to orient your new day in the direction of meaning. It is also a good idea to keep it simple. It needn't take you more than a few minutes, or even just a few seconds, to aim yourself in the direction of the meaning you intend to make on a given day.

The essence of this morning meaning practice is deciding how, where, and when you want to make meaning today. You might decide to invest two hours working on your new business or your current novel, an hour with your son in the afternoon after school, and an hour meeting with a new client. For the time that you spend running errands or watching television, you mentally pencil in "no meaning pressure" and allow yourself to relax. Your goals are twofold: to pencil in enough meaning so that your day feels meaningful and to remind yourself that the ordinariness of the rest of the day is acceptable.

Craft your morning meaning practice in any shape you like, and include features that you think will help you make and maintain meaning on that day. You might include a minute of meaning incanting; you might think about or rehearse a phrase or two from your personal vocabulary of meaning; you might check in on your self-talk and continue the work of replacing language that doesn't serve you with language that does. You can also include elements that you like from other practices: a little meditation, a little exercise, and so on.

Even though this morning meaning practice may take only a few minutes, it possesses great richness and depth. It is a genuine practice and involves regularity (we do not skip our practice because it is gloomy outside or because we are gloomy inside); simplicity (we show up with the right intention and with sufficient energy); solemnity (we are respectful of the vision we hold for ourselves as the arbiter of our life's meanings); honesty (about, for instance, how much time we intend to devote to this meaning opportunity or that meaning investment); presence (we aren't half-thinking about which bills need paying or whether the lawn needs mowing); ceremony (by, say, the way we open our meaning journal or light our candle); joy (by letting a quiet sense of joy be the background feeling of our practice); discipline (by spending extra time on our practice when life demands it); and primacy (by putting our morning meaning practice first and not letting other worthy practices such as our yoga or exercise practice supplant it).

Take some time and describe the morning meaning practice you desire. Explain to yourself how you will keep your practice simple, how you will keep yourself honest, how you will foster presence, and so on. Think about each of these elements, and picture yourself living your practice. How will you structure your morning meaning practice, and what will it include?

Here's how Barbara, a project manager, described her practice:

I've been religiously doing the morning practice. It's made a huge difference in my life. With each day's work building on previous days, I've pulled further out of acute depression. The main tool that I'm using for my meaning practice is a spiral notebook where I briefly write down any thoughts that I wake up with (ideas, issues, dreams) and where I describe the meaningful activities I'm planning for the day.

I also keep a monthly calendar page with squares large enough to record the daily meaning activities I accomplished the day before. The calendar provides an ongoing and cumulative record of the meaningful activities I actually managed to accomplish. In the journal, as I complete a meaning activity for the day, I put a broad red check mark beside it and record the amount of time I spent on it (if that's important). On the monthly calendar I write a Post-it note with my three main, ongoing goals.

At first I thought I'd focus on trying to get in one or two hours of more meaningful activities daily — more of the "want to do's." Then I realized that although I wanted more meaningful activities in my day I also had to make more meaningful the tasks I had to accomplish anyway — the "have to do's." So now I focus on both, on adding meaning to my day with special activities and on investing meaning in my ordinary activities.

As was promised, this morning practice takes only a few minutes each day (unless I write longer in the journal). What's so very important is the basic structure and routine, which is what I needed and which I haven't rebelled against so far — as I have throughout my life when I felt too boxed in. There is a logic and spaciousness to this morning meaning practice that really works for me.

Lynette, a novelist, explained:
I start my morning meaning practice the night before. I congratulate myself on what I've accomplished, and I orient myself to my future plans. Included in this orientation is a recommitment to my values and aspirations. In the morning, I take a moment to reflect on any dreams I can remember, and then I renew my commitment from the previous evening. Sometimes I include a little meditation, journaling, or sketching. I engage in a ritualized entry into my day that involves coffee, focused goal setting, and an immediate turning to my current novel.

Mark, a stay-at-home dad, described his focus on "being" rather than on "doing":
Most of the things that my days include are ordinary things such as changing diapers, making meals, doing the laundry, and going to the park when the weather is nice. Before I can even dream about adding more meaning activities to my day or going on some special meaning adventure, I have to remind myself to invest meaning in these ordinary events and to hold them in a certain way, with a kind of joy or reverence. There is nothing really more meaningful than being in the park with my two kids, and it doesn't pay me to pine for something more meaningful than that. So I use my brief morning meaning practice to remind myself that this day is fine just as it is, that it doesn't fall short on some "meaning calculator."

Mirella, a lawyer, talked about her practice as a kind of visualization:
My morning meaning practice is primarily a time of visualization. After I wake up, I sit in bed and spend five to ten minutes visualizing my day. I picture the tasks ahead

and imagine them running smoothly and efficiently. I picture my free moments, and I visualize using them to create some meaning, which on one day might mean writing a letter to my sister, on another day researching my next vacation on the Internet, and so on. On one day I might set a goal of doing some charitable work during my free time, on another day I might set as a goal getting to the gym for an hour. There is something about this seemingly ordinary process of making decisions that is very powerful and comforting, maybe because I am mindfully asserting that the letter to my sister or the charity work *is* meaningful to me. Maybe that's what "making meaning" really means!

Alex, a graduate student, described his morning meaning practice:
As a person with no religious or spiritual persuasions and no reason to believe that my concerns amount to a hill of beans, I find that I have to "explain" to myself daily why I should bother, given that the kind of research I do is very hard to pull off. My morning meaning practice is a kind of pep talk in which I point out to myself that as long as I am here I might as well act heroically and give a damn and keep trying, rather than tossing in the towel. On some days I find that I don't believe myself and can't get going. But without my morning meaning practice I know that there would be a lot more of those days! I've spent years adrift — with this morning meaning practice, it is only days and not years that I lose. That's an improvement!

Laurie, a musician, wrote:
I find a quiet place where I can meditate for five or ten minutes every morning. As I meditate, I ask myself the

question: What tiny step can I take today that will help me create meaning in my life? I simply ask the question and try not to worry about finding an answer. My brain begins to play with the question and generate answers. I sit in stillness, receiving answers and reviewing the answers as I focus on my breathing. At some point I accept one of the answers and know where I'll be making meaning on that day. Then I complete the meditation and move with strength and energy into the day.

Your morning meaning practice is the way you orient your day around your meaning needs and make daily decisions about where you want to invest meaning. Maybe you'll spend ten or fifteen minutes engaged with this orienting and deciding; maybe all you need is a split second. The goal is not to create a practice, as if the practice were the objective, but to begin your day putting meaning first and aiming yourself in the direction of authenticity.

CHAPTER 19

YOU NEGOTIATE EACH DAY

WHEN YOU LIVE as a meaning maker, each day is a special sort of negotiation. You make decisions about where you will invest meaning, how you will handle activities that hold no particular meaning, when you will take your vacations from meaning, and so on. You make a daily bargain with yourself that if you hold to your intentions you will find no reason to doubt the meaningfulness of that day. It is like saying, "If I have a healthy breakfast, somehow get through the holiday buffet at the office without overdoing it, and have just one treat this evening, I won't get down on myself about what I ate today."

You do not aim for some unattainable perfection. You recognize that the three hours you spend making phone calls to nursing homes on behalf of your ailing father should be toted up on the side of meaning, even if they feel like drudgery and even if the actual phoning makes you anxious. You accept that you need daily vacations from "the whole meaning thing" and pencil in the mystery novel you want to read or the movie you want to watch without the slightest bit of guilt. You adamantly demand of yourself that you put in that hard hour on your Internet business doing the thing that you've been avoiding, because that is your prime meaning-making activity on that day. This is not a "perfect" day as measured against some imaginary ideal, but it is a carefully negotiated day full of hard work, service, and relaxation and a day to completely accept — and be proud of.

First of all, you designate *something* as that day's meaning investment. If your job holds no meaning for you, that is a real problem, and you will have to decide if investing meaning in it, even though you don't receive the psychological experience of meaningfulness in return, is the right daily meaning investment. Maybe you will need to treat work as a chore and invest daily meaning elsewhere. If you have a job — whether it is selling insurance, writing a novel, cleaning chimneys, or caring for your home and family — you will need to make daily decisions about the way you intend to navigate that job.

On one day your negotiations might sound like, "I am investing meaning in that business meeting today — I am going to go in there fully prepared, and I'm going to follow up on whatever transpires — and then I'm going to take a vacation from meaning by catching up on that pile of nonessential emails waiting for me." On another day, your negotiations might sound like, "Nothing about work can be made to feel meaningful today, so I am going to invest meaning in the hour before work and in the hour after work and enjoy carving that crib for Mary's baby."

If no work tastes good to you, that is a terrible problem. If, to the description of every occupation in a manual of occupations, you respond, "Not that interested," that is an incipient meaning crisis. How can unhappiness not be waiting for you? Part of your daily negotiation is keeping an eye peeled for *what can be experienced as meaningful*, even though you have serious doubts that anything can rise to that level of its own accord. Part of the idea of investing meaning is the idea of lifting up work so that it rises to a place of meaningfulness.

If the work you do is a labor of love but also horribly difficult, so difficult that on most days you hate the actuality of it even as you love the idea of it, that is on its own a genuine problem. If writing your novel or composing your symphony is pure agony, how much fun is that? How can sadness not be waiting for you? Part of your daily negotiations involves *reminding yourself of the meaningfulness of your work*, even though its execution is pure agony. This sounds like, "It is going to be hell getting through today's chapter, and whatever time I manage to spend on it will count double in my meaning calculations!"

By the same token, you must reckon with your free time. You must account for both work time and nonwork time in your daily negotiations. Both can be problematic: your work can feel like drudgery, and your free time can feel empty. If you do not need to work, if nothing is required of you and you can just recline and count the clouds scudding by, that is its own existential problem. Have another gin and tonic? Send another text message? Recline another decade? How can sadness not be waiting for you?

How you manage your free time is an essential part of your daily negotiations. This might sound like, "Okay, it is Saturday. I have some errands to run and some chores I need to get done. Okay. That's a given — no need to fret about them. What about the rest of the day? I want to watch that special this evening — I know it's a silly show, but I do want to watch it! So I'll count that as my meaning vacation. Okay, I've got errands, chores, and a meaning vacation. Oh, and sex tonight! That will be fun! But...I need more meaning than that. I'd better pencil in some additional meaning. Hmm. Okay. I think I'll find my mother's recipe for curried pumpkin soup and make a pot of it. And I'll play my mother's favorite music while I cook...that will put me in quite a mood!"

Naturally your self-conversation won't sound quite this stilted! But you get the idea — that a day is a creation, not a given. Part of this negotiation process is *looking for* meaning opportunities and meaning adventures in the coming day. Say that some friends of yours have roped you into going with them to a mall and you have no interest in shopping. You find yourself in a busy shopping center where hundreds of people are rushing around you searching for bargains. You can take this as an opportunity to write a letter to your son, read a book, or do anything you deem meaningful, even though you are being serenaded by piped-in music. On the other hand, you can sit there bored, irritated, or furious; or, maybe worse, shop even though you don't care to. This junket can be a meaning opportunity — but only if you hold it that way.

Say you're attending a cocktail party. Party etiquette demands that you circulate and make small talk. Maybe your only goals for the evening are to survive the chatter, grab the good hors d'oeuvres, and get a little tipsy. What may better serve your meaning-making needs, however, is settling in with the fellow who knows everything about the career you're contemplating starting, peppering him with questions, and maybe even asking for his help. If you feel obliged to follow party rules you end up with another boring party experience. If you *take the opportunity right in front of you*, then you succeed in having a meaningful experience.

In the first case the negotiation might sound like the following: "Maybe I'll give shopping a shot and throw away twenty bucks, but as soon as that's gone I'm going to find a quiet corner — a relatively quiet corner — and write Max a long letter." In the second case the negotiation might sound like, "If there is nobody at the party who interests me or who might be of use to me, I am going home early. But if I happen upon someone interesting I'm going to monopolize that person, party etiquette be damned!"

You can plan some of this as part of your morning meaning

practice, but the rest you negotiate on the fly and in the blink of an eye. When your lover comes into the room you make the instantaneous decision to relate rather than to continue reading your book. When a squall appears on the horizon you make the instantaneous decision not to grow as dark as that squall but to opt for a feeling of contentment instead. All this happens right in the moment.

All day long you make judgments and decisions, judging, for instance, that a moment has come when you *had better* make some meaning or else risk a meaning crisis, or deciding that plenty of meaning has been made and that now you're entitled to a television show and some chocolate. You use your various techniques, such as maintaining a morning meaning practice and incanting meaning, to effectively negotiate your daily meaning challenges.

Let's look at the case of someone who appears *not* to be in any position to negotiate her day in the manner I've been describing. How, for instance, could a refugee in a refugee camp negotiate her day in any meaningful way? Isn't she too constrained by her circumstances, too obliged to keep her eye on survival, and in too great and perpetual a state of emotional upheaval to have space for a practice of this sort? Maybe she is. But maybe she isn't. What if she responds to her situation with a certain fierce pride and refuses to allow her circumstances to render her life meaningless?

Let's say that she decides to make meaning despite her circumstances, or, rather, *in* her exact circumstances. How might she negotiate her day? She can wake up and maintain a morning meaning practice just like anyone else. She can decide that she will teach her children — she can invest meaning in the activity of educating her children. She can take the meaning opportunity to love them. She can invest meaning in activism and join the camp group lobbying the international community for help.

She can negotiate her day, choosing where, when, and how to invest meaning, and she will likely feel happier than if she didn't.

She hasn't made a silk purse out of a sow's ear, and she is still a displaced person living with incredible stress. But she can do better or worse, existentially speaking, depending on whether or not she decides to actively make meaning. A coal miner, a cancer patient, a suburban housewife — all can reduce their existential difficulties by confronting their meaning challenges daily. It may not conform to their cultural norm to do so; it may prove far more difficult to do in their particular set of circumstances than if they had it easier. But meaning is still available to them.

CHAPTER 20

YOU SEIZE MEANING OPPORTUNITIES

ANYTHING CAN BE EXPERIENCED as meaningful: the look of the sky, a new family moving in down the block, a passing thought — anything, large or small. But certain meaning opportunities stand out from the rest because our species regularly experiences them as rich and valuable. We are almost guaranteed to experience life as meaningful if we invest meaning in these areas. Below are fourteen of these opportunities. As you plan your day, remind yourself that these meaning opportunities are available to you. You can wake up and say, "Toast or a bagel?" Or you can wake up and say, "What meaning opportunity should I seize today?" Which do you think does a better job of setting the stage for energy, passion, and meaning?

1. Love. We are built to experience love as meaningful. Unless life has harmed us so much that we have stopped daring to love or unless we've become so self-involved that the only love we need is self-love, love is a golden meaning opportunity. You could love today — all it takes is a softening of your heart and an object of affection. If you bestow some love today, your life will feel more meaningful. Think of some words in the family of love, such as *affection, kindness, generosity,* and *intimacy.* They paint a picture of what loving means. You can take today as an opportunity to invest meaning in loving someone or something.

2. Good works. Action makes us feel more alive. So does living our principles and values. When we marry these two ideas we get the idea of good works: real work of our own choosing that reflects our principles and our values. Maybe your everyday work feels short on real value but you must continue with it because it pays the bills. Try to supplement that everyday work with some good works of your own choosing. Your life will feel more meaningful if you pick good works as one of your meaning opportunities.

3. Creativity. Creativity is a rich, large word that stands for the way we use our resources and talents. We can approach anything creatively — creativity is not reserved for certain pursuits such as writing a novel or inventing software. Life feels richer when we turn on that inner tap and allow our natural creativity to flow. Creativity in this everyday sense is an excellent meaning opportunity. You can choose to approach some challenge at work with grudging energy and a feeling of boredom, or you can decide to invest something of yourself in meeting the challenge, bring to bear your inner resources and talents, spend a little of your passion, and attack it creatively. Life feels more meaningful when you approach it this way.

4. Excellence. As children we start out with two qualities, both of which appeal to us greatly: we love to experiment and we love to excel. Soon, though, because we're pressured to get things right, we start to lose our taste for experimentation; and because much of what we do doesn't rise to the level of excellence, we begin to fear that excellence isn't in us. Out of this dynamic arises a middle-of-the-road approach to life. Still, excellence remains a golden meaning opportunity for you. You can decide to bite into something and do it really well. Maybe you'll flounder at first; maybe you'll make some heroic messes. But if you apply yourself and if you persevere, excellence is waiting. And how good it will feel! Give excellence a chance, and add it to your list of meaning opportunities.

5. Relationships. Protecting our individuality requires that we remain separate: we can't think our thoughts or dream our dreams unless we stay in our own skins. But while separateness and solitude are precious, relationships remain golden meaning opportunities. They are the place to love and be loved; the place to befriend and be befriended; the place to make work, business, and career connections; the place to be human in the presence of other human beings. Some of these relationships are rather like traps; others are the very beauty of life. Consciously decide where you want to relate, choosing the riches and avoiding the traps, and put relating high on your list of meaning opportunities.

6. Stewardship. It is reasonable enough to focus on our own survival needs, appetites, and desires. Evolution has built that primacy right into us. But nature also has provided us with a sense of right and wrong and an understanding of ideas such as responsibility, mutuality, and shared humanity. Therefore, we feel better if we aim ourselves in the direction of stewardship: in the direction of care for and attention to the world in which we live, the creatures of this world, and the ideas and institutions that maintain civilization at its best. We can aim to steward our children, civil rights, democratic institutions, the environment, or anything small or large that we think is worth our concern. It could be the stream at the edge of town; it could be the freedom of one person to speak. Stewardship meets both our ethical and psychological needs. Pick something to steward — a person, an ideal, a resource — and life will feel more meaningful.

7. Experimentation. Many of us curtail our natural desire to experiment since, during our formative years, we are instructed in school, at home, and by our peers to get things right and not make mistakes. Often we are literally punished for experimenting, and so we lose our taste for it. However, experimenting is a core element of creativity, growth, and learning. We can't learn a new art medium unless we experiment with it. We can't learn how to run our business except through trial and error. If you've lost your taste for experimentation, see if you can reacquire it by choosing experimentation as one of your meaning opportunities. Let go of needing a successful outcome, don't worry whether you will get it right or wrong, and rejoice in the experimental process.

8. Pleasure. It goes without saying that people find pleasure a source of meaning. Yet because of familial, cultural, and religious injunctions against enjoying pleasure, or because we think that pleasure is too low a thing to honor, many people reject pleasure as a significant meaning opportunity. In a well-rounded life in which we are making meaning on many fronts, by creating, by being of service, by entering into relationships, and so on, pleasure ought to take its rightful place. If our lives were only about garnering pleasure we might justifiably feel that we had strayed too far from our principles. But if we're living a value-based life we're certainly entitled to plenty of pleasure! Pleasure is not a suspect or second-rate meaning opportunity, and *puritanical* and *meaningful* are not synonyms.

9. Self-Actualization. Self-actualization, like creativity, is a word that stands for our desire to make the most of our talents and inner resources. Instead of using only a small portion of your total being, you make the heroic decision to employ your full intelligence, your emotional capital, and your best personality qualities in the service of your meaning investments. This is hard to do. Your personality shadows may get in the way. The facts of existence may get in the way. You may want to use your full potential in the service of writing a novel, say, but that embroils you in the very real process of writing a novel, with all of its mysteries and difficulties. Despite these built-in problems, you know in your heart that you would love to actualize your potential and make yourself proud.

10. Service. Being of help feels meaningful. It is a service, for example, to make things easier rather than harder for the people around you, to hold the vision and values of your community, company, or family when that vision blurs, to spontaneously provide your expertise when your expertise is needed, and to point someone in the right direction. Some of your meaning opportunities require that you stand up for yourself and assert your individuality. Others provide you with the opportunity to share your human wealth and enter into relationship with others. Service is one of the latter. Life feels most meaningful when you honor both aspects of existence, the communal as well as the individual.

11. Career. If you're a painter, it isn't your goal to paint an occasional painting and hide it away in your attic. If you're a coach, it isn't your goal to help an occasional client and wait months or years for the next occasion to help. *Career* is the word we use to stand for our desire to work in a regular, productive, and effective way in our chosen field. Having a career isn't synonymous with making a living. A career poet can't live on the money she makes from her poetry "sales." Nevertheless, she can have a real career and many psychological and objective successes. You can turn any passion into a career by paying real attention to it and giving it a place of primacy in your life. If it evolves into a career, it may become one of your most important meaning opportunities.

12. Attitude. We create much of our own suffering by not getting a grip on our self-talk and by refusing to choose what attitudes to adopt. For example, you can keep rehashing the past and by doing so ensuring that the future resembles it — or you can be here, right now, enjoying all that there is to enjoy in the present moment. You can decide to invest meaning in your very attitude: in an attitude of mindfulness, in an attitude of contentment, in any attitude you deem desirable. Your attitude is one of your core meaning opportunities. Your life will feel more meaningful according to the attitudes you adopt and the stances you take toward life. You can turn everything into a drama, or you can let unimportant matters roll off your back. You can worry yourself into inaction, or encourage yourself to succeed. Your attitude choices significantly affect your ability to make meaning.

13. Achievement. We are built with an ego and powerful desires, and there is no reason not to honor that part of our endowment. Even if we have learned to live in a detached, phlegmatic, and philosophical way, we can still cherish achievement. We can congratulate ourselves for staying the course and for building a name for ourselves in our field, for completing large-scale projects, or for accomplishing tasks with fortitude and excellence. There is nothing paradoxical about holding both contentment and accomplishment as meaning opportunities. You can make a meaning investment in sitting contentedly by a pond soaking up the sun for this hour, and you can make a very different meaning investment the next hour by accomplishing something. You don't have to choose between "being" and "doing": you can honor both.

14. Appreciation. Many people lead gloomy, pessimistic, critical, and self-critical lives. They may have abundant reasons for living that way, but those reasons do not amount to a verdict.

Even people who have been terribly harmed still have as one of their meaning opportunities the possibility of appreciating life. Life feels more meaningful when you appreciate a juicy apple, a day of rest, an accomplishment, a child at play, or a summer breeze. You can invest meaning one minute by writing a strong letter of protest and the next by appreciating the peach pie sitting on your kitchen counter. The latter is not a small or shallow meaning opportunity.

You can make practical sense of the idea of meaning opportunities by thinking through which ones seem most valuable to you, deciding which of those you want to investigate further, and actively investing meaning in your choices. Today you might invest meaning in experimentation, tomorrow you might opt for service, and Thursday you might choose pleasure (or, of course, you might opt for some of each on the same day!). By championing the idea of meaning opportunities, you energize your experience of meaning, and you reduce your unhappiness.

CHAPTER 21

YOU HANDLE MEANING CRISES

IN PREVIOUS CHAPTERS I've described practices that help you make meaning. However, even if you get very practical at meaning-making, the occasional meaning crisis will still strike. These crises cause profound unhappiness, and it will pay huge dividends to learn how to handle them quickly and effectively.

When your subjective sense of the meaningfulness of a situation, activity, or experience moves from positive to negative, you've hit a meaning crisis. Even if you just move from positive to neutral, from a feeling of "wow!" to one of "who cares?" a crisis has struck. It is one thing to take meaning vacations or to stay in "meaning neutral" for a while. But when meaning leaks out of your life and your subjective psychological experience is no longer positive, you are obliged to restore meaning, or you will find yourself bored, unhappy, or worse — in despair.

Maybe you love reading mysteries and suddenly one day, for no reason that you can name, mysteries just don't seem meaningful to you any longer. Maybe environmental issues always have held meaning for you, but one day you notice that another species is about to become extinct — and you find that you don't care. Somehow the meaning has drained out of saving species. These shifts and changes, some of them small and some of them enormous, bring existential pain and confusion in their wake. It is vital that you learn to identify and resolve the meaning crises that inevitably and perennially confront you.

Consider the following three scenarios. In each one you have been doing something for a long time, something that once felt meaningful but no longer does. A meaning crisis has occurred: meaning has leaked out, and unhappiness has leaked in.

Scenario one: You've been teaching the same subject for the past twenty years. You like teaching, you like your students, you like the subject you teach, but mostly you have to teach to the tests, and every year you are given more duties that have nothing to do with teaching. You are now about to start your twenty-first year of teaching, and you are not really looking forward to it. Your predominant feeling is sadness mixed with fatigue.

Scenario two: You have a strong interest in bees and have been an avid beekeeper for the past fifteen years. Lately your hives have been hit hard by an inexplicable epidemic, and most of your bees have died. Now, as you are about to start your sixteenth year of beekeeping, you could start fresh with new bees — but without any guarantee that your hives won't be hit again. Your predominant feeling is sadness mixed with anxiety.

Scenario three: You are a lawyer specializing in death-row appeals. It is a branch of the law that pays very little money and that you chose on principle. However, during the decade that you've done this work virtually none of your appeals has saved an inmate from execution. You are about to start your eleventh year. Your predominant feeling is sadness mixed with anger.

What do you do in these situations? Most human beings tend to try one or another of the following seven options.

1. They deny what is going on. The teacher takes antidepressants for her "depression," focuses on hating her principal, gives her students lower grades than she has in the past, and finds herself uncontrollably sobbing at unexpected moments.

The beekeeper goes on antianxiety medication and further tries to quell his anxious feelings by going on a hunt for bees "guaranteed to survive," even though the bees he locates cost more than he can afford and he suspects he is being duped about their hardiness.

The lawyer launches angry tirades at shop clerks and waiters, seeks out therapy to help with her "anger management issues," gets sicker than she has in many years, and finds herself verbally attacking her clients, which she attributes to "dealing with a bunch of losers."

2. They consciously try to make the best of it. The teacher reminds herself that she is helping her students, even if not as much as she would like because of the narrowness of the curriculum; she gets out of bed, puts one foot in front of the other, and gets through the new school year by trying to "turn her frown upside down."

The beekeeper acknowledges his anxiety, crosses his fingers, begins with new bees, does what he has always done (because he doesn't know what to change or where the problem is), and wakes up each morning wondering how many bees he will find still alive.

The lawyer immerses herself in her next appeal, taking some comfort in the fact that her presence and her efforts reduce the pain and anxiety of clients awaiting death. She works hard to produce a brief that may do the trick, although she knows that it almost certainly won't — that "almost" being just about everything she hangs her hat on.

3. They try to reframe the situation. The teacher reminds herself that she has her vacations and summers free, congratulates herself for choosing a profession that allows her that much free time, and pledges to enjoy herself more both at school and away from school.

The beekeeper reminds himself that the natural world is exactly what it is, so little in his control that he might as well smile at the idea of controlling it, and pledges to enjoy each bee while it lasts and experience pleasure at every drop of honey he gathers.

The lawyer reminds herself that she can live, albeit modestly, on only four or five death penalty cases a year, providing her with four or five righteous challenges annually coupled with more free time than a corporate lawyer could ever dream of having.

4. They make changes that they hope will improve the situation. The teacher creates new lesson assignments that she hopes will spark some interesting class discussions and that will make the material feel fresh to her.

The beekeeper purchases, at a modest cost and from a reputable source, a strain of bees with a track record of being less susceptible to the recent epidemic.

The lawyer decides to reduce her client load from five annual cases to three so as to reduce the time she spends worried and frustrated.

5. They try something new over there while making do over here. The teacher takes some online classes in knitting so as to pursue an old love and to cheer herself up when she is not in the classroom.

The beekeeper decides to raises alpacas so as to gather fleece as well as honey.

The lawyer takes on a couple of clients whose issues do not bring her into contact with the criminal justice system.

6. They get out of the current situation without a plan in place. The teacher walks into her principal's office one cloudy morning and tells him that she is quitting.

The beekeeper suddenly takes his entire beekeeping operation to the equivalent of the dump.

The lawyer wakes up one morning and begins calling all the death-row appeals lawyers she can locate to see if any of them are willing to take over her cases.

7. They get out of the current situation with a plan in place. The teacher investigates the profession of coaching, calculates that it might take her about five years to build a practice large enough to allow her to quit teaching, and signs up for her first coaching class.

The beekeeper decides to become a lay expert on the stressors facing bees with an eye to moving from keeping bees to writing popular articles about the dangers that bees face.

The lawyer decides that she will pursue the only other area of the law that interests her, intellectual property law, and creates a plan that will allow her to make the transition over the course of a few years from death-row appeals law to intellectual property law.

Here is how one teacher, Samantha, tried to make teaching feel meaningful to her again:

For the past six years I've tried to reinvest meaning in my teaching. I've taken on new challenges and roles. I've worked harder — and I've also tried not to work as hard. I've tried to change my attitude and my expectations — this has proven the least successful. I haven't managed to change my attitude or expectations at all, no matter how many times I've tried! I've sought support by talking to my boss, trying to use my regular appraisal more productively, and problem solving with peers. I've reduced my teaching load from five days to four days to two days.

I've tried to balance my two teaching days with meaningful activities on the other days. This worked for a while, but then I realized that on the two days I did teach I still felt no better and that those two days every week amounted to days of frustration and meaninglessness. I tried to find enough meaning in my teaching job by talking to myself about job security and guaranteed income. I tried changing my mind, altering the situation, making meaning elsewhere: I've tried everything. But there's no question about it: the meaning is gone.

Mirella tried a combination of reframing and innovation: For me, being innovative means taking a step back from the expectations and associated guilt that come with being seen as not a good teacher. Since schools are often such closed communities and run on a system of goodwill, teachers are often made to feel guilty if they are not extending enough "goodwill" to their school and students (i.e., not doing enough work for free). Creating my own meaning at school meant stepping away from that mind-set and focusing just on the classroom and my own smaller microcosm.

I also tried finding and defining a new role for myself within the school by offering to teach a "making meaning class" before or after school. That went nowhere. When I realized that there wasn't really any way to innovate, I went into a tailspin. But focusing on the classroom is working decently enough these days. As long as I enjoy classroom teaching and don't fret about whether I am doing enough for the school, I may be able to keep meaning afloat here.

Leslie tried a variation of the seventh option by planning for new meaning as she withdrew meaning from her current teaching career:

As I struggled with whether or not to leave my tenured academic job, one of my issues was that though I was working in the field of my choice, which was music, I wasn't doing enough of what I wanted to be doing in that field, which was performing chamber music. After a day of teaching, furthering other people's causes, and dodging political bullets I didn't feel I had the energy to do anything personally meaningful. I was beginning to lose my love for music, and that wasn't okay with me.

I chose to give up one meaning container, academia, in order to recommit to an older but much more personally compelling meaning container, music. I created a plan and set it in motion. I quit my day job, moved to a town where I had performing connections and a better support system, started my own chamber ensemble, and started to think bigger thoughts about who I was. I started consciously thinking, "I am a pianist, I am a musician, I am an artist, I am an entrepreneur, I am a creative force, I am a work in progress, my life is just beginning" instead of "I am an associate professor, I am tenured, I am a teacher, I have financial stability and security, I have a retirement account, I have a finished life — game over."

Consider a teacher we'll call Brad. If Brad has lost the meaning in his fifteen-year high school chemistry teaching job but is passionate about musical theater, he might try some combination of options four and five by helping students write and produce a musical — say, about two characters, Hydrogen and Oxygen, and how they get together to create Water. This project would bring something that he loves into the mix, somewhat changing the focus of his day and his job. If he could pull this project off, it might constitute a sufficient answer to this meaning crisis.

But for this solution to work, all of the following must fall into place. Brad's school must be the kind of school where the chemistry teacher can double as the drama teacher (and how many schools are like that?). Brad must convince his principal that his students will not do poorly on their chemistry APs, despite the fact that he is now putting on a play (and if their scores drop for any reason, that is probably the end of Brad's theater career at that school). Brad must raise funds for props and scenery, which is a separate job from running rehearsals and putting on the play. Brad must not hate his chemistry classes even more than he did before, now that he has this exciting other thing to turn to, and find the way to tolerate teaching chemistry. Even if all this falls into place, will this picture work for Brad? Will a regimen of boring chemistry classes punctuated by three nights of performance a year work to solve his meaning problem? Who can say?

Some of our options for handling meaning crises are primarily existential in nature. Some are primarily cognitive. Some are primarily behavioral. Some are a combination of two or three of these. It is existential to remind yourself that nature is nature and that epidemics and extinctions are out of your control. It is cognitive to focus your mind on how much free time your job affords rather than on how burdensome it feels. It is behavioral to switch your law practice from one specialty to another. Every time meaning leaks away, you must decide which existential, cognitive, and behavioral tactics you are going to employ to plug the leak and restore meaning. As much as the mental health industry would like you to believe it is, neither a pill nor talk is a substitute for this kind of work. Pills and talk may help, but the work remains.

When meaning is in doubt, consult the above list of seven options. Do you want to deny what's up? Do you want to buck up? Do you want to engage in some hopeful reframing? Do you want to make small, strategic changes, seize some new meaning opportunities, or make a huge change? These are the questions. You handle the inevitable meaning crises that arise in this sensible, systematic way, by asking these questions and by trying to answer them.

CHAPTER 22

YOU ENGAGE IN EXISTENTIAL SELF-CARE

IF YOU TAKE CHARGE OF THE MEANING in your life and keep a good eye on what matters to you, and if you align your thoughts and your actions with what matters to you, you will spend your evening working on your symphony rather than avoiding it, you will imbue dinner with your mate with love, you will skip entanglements that don't serve you, you will stand up to the jabs of difficult people — in short, you will stay focused on your existential agenda and in the process minimize your experience of unhappiness.

As you become expert at existential self-care you begin to understand the extent to which you create meaning and the extent to which meaning is a deep, inexhaustible wellspring and an infinitely renewable resource. You can invest the increments of time that rise up before you with appropriate meaning: there is always another meaning available. You make it; it comes out of you; it is new each day; it is infinitely variable. You arise each morning and make your next meaning decision. When you arm yourself with your intentions and act this bravely your unhappiness can't linger.

Emmy van Deurzen explained in *Existential Counseling and Psychotherapy in Practice*:

The process of investigation and discovery that is embarked upon with a client can lead to a reordering of experience and a revelation of new ways of creating meaning. However confused and disorganized life may seem to those who believe themselves to be adrift on a sea of contradictions and chaos, it is always possible to find clarity and order for those who believe life to be basically meaningful. The existential position is neither that of belief in chaos nor that of belief in order. It is that of belief in people's ability to create meaning and order, in spite of seeming chaos and absurdity.

You want that belief for yourself. You want to champion meaning and wake up each morning ready to invest meaning. The challenge isn't so much *where* you invest meaning but rather that you create a life anchored by regular experiences of meaningfulness. Today you might invest meaning in something outlandishly grand, and tomorrow you might invest it in something as quiet as tending your garden or as unremarkable as removing items from your to-do list. If you keep your life purposes in mind and make decisions based on your understanding of what authentic living entails, the "what to invest in" will follow. Each day you wake up ready to honor your intention to live purposefully.

What does this sound like in the living? Barbara, a writer, described how she invests meaning:
The idea that we are responsible for making meaning in our lives speaks deeply to me. I think that the concept of searching for or finding meaning has stood in the way of my creative work. The ideas of making meaning, investing meaning, divesting meaning, meaning crisis, meaning drain, and so on make total sense to me. As I look back at the periods in my life when I have been

assailed by depression, each moment entailed a meaning crisis. I had invested meaning in a given relationship or activity that ceased to have meaning. I had the mistaken notion that the investment of meaning was permanent, so when the meaning drained away, I was left in despair and blamed myself for it. I now realize that just as I choose to invest meaning, I can also choose to divest meaning instead of feeling that somehow I failed. How freeing that is!

I thought that I was "supposed" to write a certain nonfiction book because it was "worthy." I thought that it should be meaningful, but it actually wasn't, which drained energy from my ability to write anything. So I have divested meaning from that project (wish I had done that two years ago!) and am continuing with my mystery writing, where the juice actually is. Writing fiction is much more energizing and freeing for me than the nonfiction project. My mind circles around possibilities — settings, characters, plot — and I can feel my energy increasing. For now, I am investing meaning in my mystery series — and that feels just right. That is where I can best make meaning at this time!

Yet the feeling of resolution you get from Barbara's report shouldn't lead you to believe that meaning is now settled in Barbara's life. In fact, all of the following happened subsequent to this report: She wrote a mystery, could not find a publisher for it, returned to nonfiction, did not find nonfiction any more meaningful this time around, started a second mystery in the series but couldn't maintain motivational energy, moved on to short stories, a genre that felt rich and that opened the door to a literary novel, the project that she is now pursuing.

You can tell just how many ups and downs must have

accompanied this ride! But because of her commitment to the idea of making meaning, she moved relatively painlessly from one meaning investment to the next. Were there days of doubt and blueness? Certainly. Did she pine for the facts of existence to be different and for the universe to be friendlier to her mystery? Naturally. But did she sink, as so many writers in her position have sunk, into despair? She did not.

Existential self-care consists of grounding yourself in a pair of realities: that life is exactly as it is and that you are obliged to keep your head up and make yourself proud. Most people make the mistake of supposing that if they don't look life squarely in the eye they can avoid noticing what is making them unhappy. Instead, they simply increase their unhappiness. By accepting the realities of life, by announcing that you intend to direct life as best you can, and by asserting that what matters to you is what you decide matters to you, you stand up straight — and that gesture does wonders for your mood and your experience of life.

We long for life to "finally settle down" and stop throwing us meaning curveballs. We want not to repeat our mistakes, not to make whopping new mistakes, not to stand before life not knowing what to do next, and not to experience serious doubts and anxieties. But life can't settle down, existentially speaking. Tomorrow I may lose a parent or a child — that may change everything. Tomorrow I may start on something more ambitious than anything I've ever tackled before — naturally I'll doubt, grow anxious, and make mistakes! We want something like a guarantee out of life: if I reach a certain age or a certain stage I can finally stand in a place of certitude. But only death brings *that* certitude. Life brings new questions and new challenges.

Frederick Karl and Leo Hamalian describe the central theme

running through the eighteen stories they include in *The Existential Imagination*:

> Man experiences an encounter with nothingness — whether it be internal or external — and either succumbs to it or overcomes it through some personal resolution...man has to transcend his pettiness and become a "hero." He is obliged to become worthy of his existence, and his worthiness derives from his confrontation with his situation, no matter how disenchanting, no matter how difficult and frustrating. Existential fiction is painful for the very reason that it strips life of its deceptions, while even the most realistic of us tend to hold to some illusions and believe them necessary.

Who wouldn't be inclined to cling to illusions and self-deceptions in the face of reality? If only we had considerably less consciousness! But we have the consciousness we have, and the main challenge that existential self-care addresses is the challenge of consciousness itself. We have consciousness of many things: our pain and the pain of others; the fragility of life; the reality of evil; the misery that people make for each other; the success of others; the ordinariness of most pursuits; the ignominy of bills to pay and day jobs to survive; the certainty of losses to come, mistakes to be made, and blows to endure.

We are aware of a million things, from the extra weight we're carrying to the inexorable crawl of time. In a single day we see villainy rewarded, a new flu spreading, our important work avoided, and our skin sagging. We just can't seem to look that much truth in the eye. It is simply too much to bear — or so we think. But to opt for blinkers is not the answer. The answer is to remain steadfastly conscious and to exercise existential self-care. You counteract consciousness with *more* consciousness

— you fight fire with fire. You announce that not only are you conscious of *all that*, but you are also conscious of your ability to heroically champion your intentions.

You are obliged to designate yourself as the arbiter of meaning in your life. You actively make meaning, you keep your meaning intentions in mind by creating a life-purpose vision, you adopt a personal vocabulary of meaning, and you maintain a morning meaning practice. You adopt the attitudes and engage in the practices we've been discussing. You make explicit the relationship you intend to have with life, one full of value and effort. And you engage in cognitive and behavioral self-care, the subjects of the next two chapters.

CHAPTER 23

YOU ENGAGE IN COGNITIVE SELF-CARE

WHAT YOU THINK determines how you feel. It is up to you to get a grip on your mind so that you do not make yourself miserable. Your thoughts do not constitute some sort of truth. They are just thoughts. They may have arisen for no good reason whatsoever. A cloud passes in front of the sun, and you think, "Life is meaningless." What sort of thought is that? Why should you feel obliged to countenance it? Why even give it the time of day? It is a terrible mistake to take thoughts at their face value, as if they arrive from on high. They just come from you, with all your warts and agendas.

If a thought serves you, you keep it. If it doesn't serve you, you reject it. If you think, "I'm spending the next two hours making meaning," you keep it. If you follow that thought with, "But maybe I'm on the wrong track and maybe I've made a mess of my life," you reject it instantly, without muss or fuss. You say, "Wow, that follow-up thought was a whopper! The heck with it." It is completely on your shoulders to accept or reject your thoughts. Who else is in a position to do that for you?

If the key existential solution to the problem of human sadness is to embrace the idea of meaning as a renewable resource and, as a consequence of that embrace, to look forward to each new day as an opportunity to make meaning, the key cognitive solution is to assert that your thoughts are yours to accept or reject and that you will think in ways that do not promote sadness. You can't just think whatever you want, any more than you can just behave any way you want. Make your thoughts align with your intentions.

Many people do a poor job of getting an adequate grip on their minds and fail to realize that their thoughts are "thinking them." They are slaves to their thoughts and may spend their whole lives never once stepping back and asking the obvious question, "Am I *obliged* to think this?" It is a form of grandiosity to presume that every thought you think is a pearl. It may seem strange to imagine that thinking "I have no talent" or "I am so depressed" is a form of grandiosity, but it is. If you take every thought you think at face value, what you are saying is "all of my thoughts are right." Isn't that the height of narcissism?

Thoughts must be *examined*. That's what the existential ideal demands. You must not let yourself get away with thoughts that do not serve you, that prevent you from making meaning, that deride you or derail you, or that arise because some martyr or trickster lurks within you. It would be better if you did not have thoughts that don't serve you — it would be better, that is, if they never bubbled up in the first place. But when they *do* bubble up, it is your job not to nod in unthinking agreement. You must actively choose the thoughts to keep and the ones to discard.

One branch of psychotherapy that does keep its eye on this essential aspect of mental health is cognitive therapy. Because cognitive therapists focus on the idea of "thinking as choice," clients of cognitive therapists tend to find the advice they receive sensible and applicable. When a cognitive therapist explains the different kinds of cognitive distortions that afflict people, their explanations make sense because they match a client's felt experience. Although psychotherapy is "only talk" and not medicine or science, <u>focusing on getting a better grip on</u> <u>your mind is an essential part of banishing sadness.</u>

Cognitive therapists tend to have a good handle on how our thoughts create our unhappiness. For example, Matthew McKay, Martha Davis, and Patrick Fanning explain in *Thoughts and Feelings*:

> It has been demonstrated over and over that most pain-ful emotions are immediately preceded by some kind of <u>interpreting thought</u>. For example, a new acquaintance doesn't telephone when he said he would. If your inter-preting thought is, "He doesn't like me after all," you would feel sad at being rejected. If your thought was, "He's been in a car crash," you would feel anxiety for his well-being. If you thought, "He deliberately lied to me about calling," you might feel anger at his falsehood. This simple insight forms the heart of cognitive behav-ioral therapy: <u>You can change your feelings by changing</u> <u>your thoughts.</u>

These interpreting thoughts are not unlike schoolkids rush-ing through the halls without supervision. Where is the hall monitor? Where is the voice inside you that asks, "How does this line of thinking serve me?" It is one thing to have a passing thought like "I wouldn't mind getting high tonight" or "Every-body has better connections than I do" flit through your mind. But having it flit through your mind and taking it seriously are two different things. You do not accept it at face value until you have looked at it and judged it. *Thoughts have to pass muster.*

Because cognitive therapists focus on the useful area of mal-adaptive self-talk, when a cognitive therapist gives a client homework — for example, that he listen to what he says to himself, that he dispute those thoughts that don't serve him, and that he substitute more useful language for the banished thoughts — the client is likely to understand the task and, if he does the work, find it helpful. It is easy to appreciate the tactics and strategies of cognitive therapy because, by having oriented itself around the idea of cognitive mistakes, it involves clients in exactly the right sort of conversation.

What sorts of techniques do cognitive therapists suggest? Aaron Beck et al. explain in *Cognitive Therapy of Depression*:

> [The cognitive] approach consists of highly specific learning experiences designed to teach the patient the following operations: (1) to monitor his negative, automatic thoughts (cognitions); (2) to recognize the connections between cognition, affect, and behavior; (3) to examine the evidence for and against his distorted automatic thought; (4) to substitute more reality-oriented interpretations for these biased cognitions; and (5) to learn to identify and alter the dysfunctional beliefs which predispose him to distort his experiences.

When a client engages in this sort of work he discovers just how much his thoughts have been ruining his mood.

Human beings make all sorts of cognitive mistakes that create and maintain sadness. One is using language to slam shut the door on possibility. Once you say, for example, "My life sucks," you've ended the conversation. After you tell yourself such a thing, is it conceivable that anything but unhappiness would follow? When you say, "My life sucks," there is nothing left to do but get drunk, hide under the covers, seek your revenge, or in some other way live defeated. Your thought has stripped you of hope and a sense of possibility.

You may feel that your life sucks, but you are not free to unleash that thought and let it run through the halls of your mind like a banshee. The feeling may sit like a lump in your chest, but the thought is there for you to scrutinize and to interrogate. How do you interrogate it? By asking, "How does this thought serve me?" The question isn't whether a thought like "My life sucks" is irrational or unreasonable. The question is whether or not it serves you. That is the measure of any thought you think — does it serve you in your efforts to earn the experience of authenticity?

A thought may be true but also not be of any use to you. It may be true that most new businesses fail. That thought, if you think it just to pester yourself and predict failure, does not serve you. It may be true that your neighbor is beautiful. That thought, if you think it to precipitate an affair or to create a longing, does not serve you. It may be true that a billion people are starving. That thought, if you think it to judge life a cheat or to take your mind off the hard work in front of you, does not serve you. Just because a thought may be true does not make it necessary. It is only useful if it *is* useful.

Very often an unproductive thought follows on the heels of a productive one, rising up from within you because something about your productive thought disturbed you. Maybe you finally commit to speaking up about something that's been on your mind — and the thought greatly frightens you the instant you think it. So you follow up the thought "I will speak!" with the thought "but Mark is going to be in an especially foul mood tonight because it's Tuesday." You quickly find the reason not to speak tonight, you undo your resolve, and you fail to live authentically.

Maybe you finally decide to practice the piano — and the thought of practicing as many hours as it would take to sound decent exhausts you even as you think it. So you follow up the thought "I'd love to practice the piano!" with "I'm much too old to learn complicated piano music." The second thought is not only objectively false but not even what you were thinking or feeling. It is a convenient dodge, a way to let you off the hook, and an invitation to guilt and regret.

The first step in cognitive self-care is clearly hearing each thought you think and willing yourself to examine it. The second step is to say, "I don't want this thought!" to all the unproductive ones. In cognitive therapy, this is called "thought confrontation." Without hesitation or embarrassment, you say, "No!" The third step is to replace the unproductive thought with a useful one (which in many cases might be your favorite meaning incantation). In cognitive therapy, this is called "thought substitution." Practice this enough, and unproductive thoughts may not even bother to arise, knowing from experience that they are just going to be banished as soon as they appear.

You may be thinking, Isn't there some deeper work to do than just dismissing thoughts that don't serve me? Don't I want to know where those thoughts come from and why they keep returning? Maybe you do; and maybe you don't. Depth therapists and analytic therapists would say that you do need to know, while cognitive therapists and behavioral therapists would say that you don't really. You will have to decide. But even if you decide that "going deep" isn't necessary, you must conclude that doing this in-the-moment work *is* necessary. A substantial portion of the unhappiness you experience occurs because you allow thoughts that do not serve you to linger. Use the power you possess to banish them.

At a writers' conference a writer asked me, "Can I really do that? Can I get rid of thoughts I've been thinking my whole life and replace them with new ones?" I replied, "If you want to." You may not want to for any number of reasons. In that case, you won't. You will keep your current thoughts and the unhappiness they engender. The Age of Reason became the Age of Anxiety in large part because too few people thought to ask whether they should countenance all their thoughts just because they thought them. Having thoughts, rather than thinking, became prized. You can change all that — if you want to.

Make the fantastic leap to the idea that you can own your own mind. Refuse to accept that you are a prisoner of your thoughts. Refuse to accept that you are condemned to repeat the same negative thoughts and the same unproductive ways of thinking. Decide to make conscious decisions about how and what you want to think. Extinguish language that supports your sadness, speak to yourself in productive ways, and then align your behaviors with your upgraded way of thinking.

CHAPTER 24

YOU ENGAGE IN BEHAVIORAL SELF-CARE

YOU CREATE INTENTIONS, you align your thoughts with those intentions — and then you behave in ways that are aligned with your intentions. You actually decide how you will behave. You decide that you will drink less or not at all, and then you drink less or not at all. You decide that you will eat, even though part of you is stubbornly anorexic, and then you eat. You decide that you will do a whole series of scary things, because each one is a necessary step in your plan to live with integrity, and then you tackle them one by one. You make meaning by creating intentions, and then you act in ways that are aligned with those intentions.

Consider the following parable. A painter opens his email and is thrilled to find a note from a gallery owner who runs a nice gallery in a faraway city. The note explains that the gallery owner has visited the painter's website, loves the painter's work, but can't find the painter's prices posted. What, the gallery owner wonders, are the artist's prices?

This question sends the artist into a tizzy, since he has no idea if the prices he has in mind are perhaps ridiculously high or, quite possibly, ridiculously low. He stews about the matter for several days, feeling his usual lack of confidence grow exponentially. Finally he visits his best friend, a successful artist with a great deal of confidence. "What should I do?" the painter cries. "I know I'm blowing this opportunity by not replying, but I don't know what to say!"

His friend shakes his head and laughs. "Give me the gallery's phone number," he says. The painter does that. His friend picks up the phone, dials, and says, "I represent Jack Sprat. You emailed him about his prices? We are setting new prices this year and would love your input. His recent works, the ones you saw on his site, are each two feet by three feet. How would you consider pricing them?" The painter watches as his friend listens, occasionally nods, and finally says, "Thanks! We'll follow up on that in a day or two."

When his friend hangs up, the painter almost leaps on him. "What did he say?" he cries. "That he would be inclined to charge $4,800 retail," his friend replies, "and that he would like to try out two of your paintings, the blue one and the red one." The painter is beside himself with joy. Then, suddenly, he exclaims, "How did you *do* that? You just picked up the phone and called!" At this, his friend shakes his head. "Jack," he replies, "how could you *not* do that? What were you thinking?"

You don't always have to do something out in the world in order to feel less sad. Sometimes you need to recalibrate your relationship to life. Sometimes you need to speak to yourself in ways that support the mood you want. But much of the time you will need to do actual things out in the world in order to feel less sad. If your personality stands in the way of your doing what you know needs to be done, you must upgrade your personality. If tradition stands in the way of your doing what needs to be done, you must break with tradition. If habit stands in the way of your doing what needs to be done, you create a new habit. If you know that you are required to take action, you must act.

Cognitive therapists, who understand that you are what you think, are also usually behavioral therapists, because they know that you are what you do as well. To reduce your experience of unhappiness you need to "think right" — and then you must act in ways that support your corrected thinking. To help clients alter and improve their behaviors, cognitive therapists suggest all sorts of tactics and strategies: that a client rehearse new behaviors in her mind's eye, that she keep a behavioral notebook to record behaviors, and so on. They know that talking about action is not enough; clients must act, if their new thinking is to matter.

Here is a brief description of the methods of behavioral therapy from MentalHelp.net:

> The behavioral aspect of CBT [cognitive-behavioral therapy] involves replacing behaviors that are contributing to patients' depression with healthier ones. CBT therapists determine whether patients' behaviors are problematic or if they appear to have skill or coping deficits. Therapists then recommend alternative behaviors as appropriate, and educate patients in missing skill sets.... CBT therapists may also use other techniques including role-playing (practicing new behaviors in session), prescription risk-taking activities (practicing new behaviors outside the therapy session), assertiveness training, and so on.

Cognitive-behavioral therapists demand that their clients work — in session and out of session. In session, "cognitive rehearsal" is a favorite tool. First you picture the action you intend to take in the real world in your mind's eye, preparing yourself for the encounter, as explained at Healthline.com: "[With] cognitive rehearsal the patient imagines a difficult situation, and the therapist guides him through the step-by-step process of facing and successfully dealing with it. The patient then works on practicing, or rehearsing, these steps mentally. Ideally, when the situation arises in real life, the patient will draw on the rehearsed behavior to address it."

Among the therapies, cognitive-behavioral therapy is singularly successful because it is talk of the right sort. It is talk about what you ought to be thinking and how you ought to be acting. As Charles Barber explains in *Comfortably Numb*: "Cognitive-behavioral therapy has been shown to be 'as effective and possibly more effective' than drugs in managing mild to moderate depression. For people suffering from moderate to even severe depression, CBT can be as effective as medications....It also has no side effects — unless you count the homework. (This is meant as a joke, but not really — the fact is that CBT requires real effort, focus, and resolve.)"

We are ready to turn the central ideas of the preceding two chapters and of this chapter into three questions around which you can orient your life:

1. What matters to me?
2. Are my thoughts aligned with what matters to me?
3. Are my actions aligned with what matters to me?

Orienting your life around these three questions forces you to live existentially, keeps your focus off your mood and on your intentions, and gives you the best possible chance to earn your experience of authenticity. Of course it isn't easy to know what matters to you or to keep your thoughts and your actions aligned with what matters to you. We've discussed the very real difficulties and constraints that get in the way of answering these three questions. Despite these difficulties and constraints, even just trying to use these three questions as a guide in organizing your life is an enormous step in the direction of integrity.

If you do use these three questions as a guide, you will join the small group of people who accept that the universe is not designed to care about them, who make peace with that realization and thus reduce their existential sadness, who make decisions about how they want to live and align their thoughts with those decisions, and who actually live that way, negotiating each day so that it holds meaning. You live according to the principle of personal pride: you live in a way that makes you proud of the "you" that you are manifesting.

Acting from pride and making yourself proud are two different ideas. Of course we're talking about the latter. Indeed, you may have to humble yourself in order to make yourself proud, say, by admitting that your drinking is out of control or by recognizing that the way you relate to people belittles them. The existential ideal is not about providing cover for arrogance, grandiosity, and narcissism. It is about demanding that you make use of your freedom to align your actions with a vision of how you intend to live authentically.

You may fall out of love. You may cycle through more than one mistaken career. You may experience unaccountable urges and serious nightmares. These events and circumstances will make you sad. Because you are sad, it will be hard to take action. However, taking action is exactly what will make you feel less sad. You want to behave in ways that support your intention to feel less sad. You want to stop behaviors that promote sadness. You want to experiment with new behaviors that you think will improve your situation and, as a result, reduce your experience of sadness. This is how you make yourself proud.

You are bound to take vacations from meaning, since every minute of the day can't be made to feel meaningful. But you try not to take vacations from personal pride. In order to survive, you may decide to do things that do not make you proud. Out of fear you may fail to speak up. Out of sloth and carelessness you may waste a day, a year, or a decade. To save your skin you may harm another. But at least you will know that you are violating your own prime directive. You will feel guilt and know to do better next time.

You take seriously the inherent difficulties in dealing with the competing forces that want a voice in answering the question, "What matters to me?" It may, for example, matter to you to live with integrity, and it may also matter to you that, say, you have a career as a police officer. What do you do when your partner, who is also your training officer, is brutal and corrupt? Do you risk ruining your career by turning him in? Do you do nothing? Do you do something in between? — and if so, what? Maybe you talk to a trusted friend — but that can't be the complete answer. Maybe you meditate, maybe you consult a therapist, maybe you take medication for what you are now calling your "depression" — but those aren't answers. What *will* you do?

Asking and then trying to answer these three questions is not a walk in the park. You do not remove life's difficulties by virtue of the fact that you have a method for living. If you aren't permitted to behave in ways that align with your intentions, a conflict exists — and maybe even a crisis. The battle may be internal, between a desire and a value. The battle may be external, between a value and a fact of existence. These battles do not go away because you are armed. *But at least you are armed.* You will at least get an A for effort — or rather, for authenticity.

Behavioral self-care is the art and practice of acting in ways that align with your intentions. It is a continual self-reminding that you are in charge of your actions, necessarily constrained as they are by the facts of existence. You can't put out a forest fire by spitting on it. You can't, despite how lovely we find the image, stop a flood by shoving your finger in the dike. But day in and day out you can act in ways that amount to real effort. That is the most you can ask of yourself; that is the least you can ask of yourself.

CONCLUSION

CRACKING THE DEPRESSION CODE

WHY IS IT that so many lottery winners, after a brief period of euphoria, become unhappier than they were before winning the lottery? This happens because there is no lottery to win with regard to life. If you were an alcoholic before you won the lottery, you are still an alcoholic — albeit with a better-stocked liquor cabinet. If you were a cranky, critical, angry young man with a hefty sense of grandiosity and no willingness to do any real work, you are still that narcissist — probably even more so. If you wanted to create symphonies, occasionally tried, but invariably bored yourself with your efforts, you could now hire a symphony orchestra to play your music — and bore a concert hall full of people. Where is the change or improvement in any of that?

This is what many lottery winners experience. If you weren't living an authentic life before you won the lottery, an influx of money will provide you with the perfect opportunity to live just as inauthentically, or even more inauthentically. If you haven't created yourself in your own best image, if you haven't demanded of yourself that you strive to understand what matters to you, if you haven't aligned your thoughts and behaviors with your intentions, an influx of money is just an opportunity to further refrain from stepping up to the plate.

So is a regimen of antidepressants. Even if you believe that there is a "mental disorder" called "depression" and that certain treatments work to minimize it or "cure" it, you must agree that you will not have cured *life* once you have cured your depression. You might cure your depression and still not be able to conjure up a single reason to go to the office, your paycheck excepted, or a way to reconcile your mate's protestations of loyalty with his affairs. Don't your human challenges remain, even if you have cured your depression? And mustn't you dream up solutions *for them*?

Human beings experience unhappiness. The typical person experiences unhappiness not only for all the usual reasons — that his teeth sometimes ache, that his job is relentlessly stressful, that his family life is no white-picket-fence heaven, and so on — but also because, as a modern person, he can't maintain the illusion that his place in the universe is particularly exalted. His life produces unhappiness, and his understanding of his place in the universe produces its own poignant unhappiness.

The former he is taught to call "depression," and the latter, if he knows the lingo, he calls "existential depression." Society's widespread willingness to believe that the "mental disorder of depression" exists produces a new set of expectations. People have come to believe that unhappiness is an aberration and that if they are experiencing it they have somehow "caught something" almost embarrassing to catch, like an STD. Who should be unhappy nowadays, what with malls and television? So, rather than admit that they are unhappy, they opt to treat their feelings like a disease. This enormously pleases Big Doctor, who welcomes each "depressive" with open arms.

Big Doctor and his ideas are everywhere, providing tremendous cover for inauthenticity. David Karp argues in *Speaking of Sadness*: "A necessary condition for widespread depressive illness is a culturally induced readiness to view emotional pain as a disease requiring medical intervention. The grounds for interpreting pain as an abnormal medical condition have been largely established through the increasing incursion of medical and other therapeutic experts into literally every aspect of our lives." Their fellow doctors, loath to rock the boat and point a finger, provide cover for their mental health brethren — they attend the same banquets, travel on the same junkets, and lend their moral support to the medicalization of sadness.

This new belief that life shouldn't hurt, a belief fostered by Big Doctor at every turn, is very strange. It is very strange that, having been sexually molested as a child, you should somehow believe that you will not experience that harm as hurtful, injurious, even ruinous. Shame a child, scare a child, belittle a child, dismiss a child, lie to a child, and what do you imagine you will produce? Happiness? It is as if we have come to be *surprised* by our feelings of unhappiness, so surprised that we involuntarily exclaim, "Wow, something must be going on. This isn't *natural*."

Nothing could be *more* natural. What sort of creature do we think we are? A kind of wishful thinking has washed over the developed world that life has become simple and settled. Aside from the occasional economic downturn, natural disaster, and unfortunate "disorder," modern life is like a good supermarket: abundant, orderly, unblemished, and brought to you with a smile. Your child would be as happy as a clam if only it weren't for her pesky attention deficit disorder and childhood depression. Your mother would be a happy old lady if only she didn't suffer from "nursing home syndrome" and "seasonal affective disorder." If only we could shed the rough coat of this or that disorder, this new story goes, we would find ourselves wearing silk pajamas.

This is a false view of life. Life is a project. The moment they are born people are dropped into a world that makes many demands and certain allowances. Either you equip yourself to deal with human unhappiness and the rigors of living, or you will find yourself dealing with them in ways that make you even unhappier. One excellent way to deal with your life-as-project is the way that I've been describing: by following an existential program that focuses on your ability to create the psychological experience of meaning. If you happen not to like my program, create your own. It won't suffice to do nothing.

Has the "mental disorder of depression" been fabricated by the mental health industry to turn human unhappiness and the consequences of human unhappiness into a cash cow? You will have to draw your own conclusions. You will have to decide what sorts of information the phrases *depression as psychological disorder* and *depression as biological disorder* are supposed to convey. You will have to decide if something has been identified or created out of whole cloth. You will have to decide if all this mental health labeling is a marvel of medical progress or a variation on the age-old human penchant for selling snake oil.

Tens of thousands of mental health professionals disagree with my position, stand behind the logic and legitimacy of the diagnostic manual they use, assert that depression is a genuine mental disorder, and advocate for antidepressants and/or psychotherapy. You may decide to agree with them — but not, I hope, because there are so many of them out there. Let their evidence and their arguments convince you, and not their numbers! And remember, as many as there are, quite a few voices are arrayed against them.

Allan Horwitz and Jerome Wakefield conclude in *The Loss of Sadness*: "Sadness is an inherent part of the human condition, not a mental disorder. Thus to confront psychiatry's invalid definition of depressive disorder is also to consider a painful but important part of our humanity that we have tended to shunt aside in the modern medicalization of human problems." In order to deal with those real problems, I am suggesting, an existential program is the best answer. It is not that the problems do not exist. But only an individual human being can answer them — and only for herself.

You set the bar. You define your terms. You skip right past viewing the universe as an inhospitable place and life as a cheat and decide that your best chance of answering the question, "How shall I live?" is by frankly *answering it*. To ask that question, shake your head, and sink back on the sofa, and to repeat that forlorn gesture so often that you almost can't help but buy the idea of depression, is not an answer. The answer is raising your hand and providing an answer. Your answer will be incomplete, contingent, worrisome, and all of that — but it will contain your life force.

You can't make all the meaning you want. You can't provide yourself with a continual experience of meaningfulness. Authenticity is not like a ladder you climb, like a ladder to success, where finally one day y sess all the authenticity you need. Authenticity is about trying, day in and day out, in the small gestures and in the big decisions you make, to live out the vision you have for yourself and to earn the experience, if only on that day and for that day, of having lived authentically.

There is no journey from unhappiness to authenticity, as if unhappiness were something that could be left behind in the dust. You live authentically, and sometimes you are unhappy. Maybe you even remain chronically and profoundly unhappy, because the harm done to you can't be healed or because you can't reconcile your reality with your dreams. Maybe you will want to take drugs for this pain, because drugs have effects; maybe you will want to talk to someone with the training to listen. However, when you feel this way and employ these methods, will you have "the mental disorder of depression"? No. Big Doctor would like you to think so — but I hope that by now you know better.

The existential program I've described is my vision. It is my subjective response to what I see as the demands posed on individuals by the facts of existence. You may see life in a very different way and not share my vision. If, however, you experience the thing called "depression" and feel like exploring an existential approach to climbing out of that hole, give my program a try. The word *depression* is a corruption of language, and the more society uses it, the further it will push us all toward unhappiness. Pathologizing unhappiness creates unhappiness. Reject the very idea of depression and make meaning instead.

NOTES

All websites accessed in June 2011.

4   *"'Medicalization' describes a process..."*: Peter Conrad, *The Medicalization of Society: On the Transformation of Human Conditions into Treatable Disorders* (Baltimore: Johns Hopkins Press, 2007), 4.

4   *"Many of the conditions encompassed..."*: Allan Horwitz, *Creating Mental Illness* (Chicago: University of Chicago Press, 2003), 15.

10   *"I would offer that what would otherwise..."*: Mel Schwartz, "The Pathologizing of a Culture," *Psychology Today* blog. Available at http://www.psychologytoday.com/blog/shift-mind/200902 /the-pathologizing-culture.

11   *"In 2002, 16 percent of the citizens of Winterset..."*: Charles Barber, *Comfortably Numb: How Psychiatry Is Medicating a Nation* (New York: Vintage Books, 2008), 5–6.

14   *"a clinically significant behavioral or psychological syndrome..."*: American Psychiatric Association, quoted in *Encyclopedia of Mental Disorders.* Available at http://www.minddisorders.com /Del-Fi/Diagnosis.html.

16   *"Even if it was shown..."*: Lawrence Stevens, "The Myth of Biological Depression." Available at http://www.antipsychiatry .org/depressi.htm.

17   *"Many of the diagnoses of mood disorder today..."*: Edward Shorter, *Before Prozac: The Troubled History of Mood Disorders in Psychiatry* (New York: Oxford University Press, 2008), 3.

27 *An elegant experiment performed by psychologist Maurice Temerlin:* Maurice Temerlin, "Suggestion Effects in Psychiatric Diagnosis," *Journal of Nervous and Mental Disease* 147, no. 4 (1968): 349–53.

28 *An excellent experiment run by Ellen Langer:* Ellen Langer and Robert Abelson, "A Patient by Any Other Name: Clinician Group Difference in Labeling Bias," *Journal of Consulting and Clinical Psychology* 42, no. 1 (1974): 4–9.

29 *"A dark truth became visible…":* Robert Whitaker, *Mad in America: Bad Science, Bad Medicine, and the Enduring Mistreatment of the Mentally Ill* (New York: Basic Books, 2002), 265.

31 *"Just because antidepressants are popular…":* Mark Hyman, "Why Antidepressants Don't Work for Treating Depression," *Huffington Post*, April 24, 2010. Available at http://www.huffingtonpost.com /dr-mark-hyman/depression-medication-why_b_550098.html.

32 *"Reboxetine, an antidepressant sold by Pfizer…":* "Reboxetine Ineffective, Drug Maker Suppressed Negative Studies, Report Says," *NewsInferno*, October 13, 2010. Available at http://www .newsinferno.com/pharmaceuticals/reboxetine-ineffective-drug -maker-suppressed-negative-studies-report-says/.

32 *"Unless patients continue taking the drugs…":* Sharon Begley, "New Hope for Battling Depression," *Wall Street Journal*, January 6, 2004. Available at http://psychrights.org/research/Digest /Effective/WSJ_comPsychotherapy.htm.

32 *"A small but vocal minority of researchers…":* Maia Szalavitz, "Antidepressants: Are They Effective or Just a Placebo?," *Time*, June 3, 2010. Available at http://www.time.com/time/health /article/0,8599,1991841,00.html.

33 *"In clinical practice, many people…":* John Kelley, "Antidepressants: Do They 'Work' or Don't They?," *Scientific American*, March 2, 2010. Available at http://www.scientificamerican.com/article .cfm?id=antidepressants-do-they-work-or-dont-they.

33 *"While Prozac was originally approved for depression…":* Peter Breggin, *Talking Back to Prozac* (New York: St. Martin's, 1995), 4.

36 *"When I suggest that psychotherapy is a myth…":* Thomas Szasz, *The Myth of Psychotherapy: Mental Healing as Religion, Rhetoric and Repression* (Syracuse, NY: Syracuse University Press, 1988), 3–4.

37   *"Just as striking to me…"*: Daniel Carlat, *Unhinged: The Trouble with Psychiatry — A Doctor's Revelations about a Profession in Crisis* (New York: Free Press, 2010), 4–5.

51   *"From [the perspective of Freud and Schopenhauer]…"*: Joshua Dienstag, *Pessimism: Philosophy, Ethic, Spirit* (Princeton, NJ: Princeton University Press, 2009), 92.

56   *"There is a crucial and inescapable distinction…"*: Maurice Friedman, *The Worlds of Existentialism: A Critical Reader* (Chicago: University of Chicago Press, 1964), 9.

116   *Howard Gardner, the originator of this:* Howard Gardner, *Multiple Intelligences: New Horizons in Theory and Practice* (New York: Basic Books, 2006).

117   *When Daniel Goleman proposed:* Daniel Goleman, *Emotional Intelligence: Why It Can Matter More Than IQ*, 10th anniversary edition (New York: Bantam, 2006).

118   *"Existential intelligence (EI) was proposed…"*: Branton Shearer, "Development and Validation of a Scale for Existential Thinking." Available at www.miresearch.org/files/Existential _AERA_Propsoal-05.doc.

188   *"The process of investigation and discovery…"*: Emmy van Deurzen, *Existential Counseling and Psychotherapy in Practice* (London: Sage Publications, 2002), 6.

191   *"Man experiences an encounter…"*: Frederick Karl and Leo Hamalian, *The Existential Imagination* (New York: Premier Books, 1963), 31.

195   *"It has been demonstrated over and over…"*: Matthew McKay, Martha Davis, and Patrick Fanning, *Thoughts and Feelings: Taking Control of Your Moods and Your Life* (Oakland, CA: New Harbinger Publications, 2007), 4.

196   *"[The cognitive] approach consists of highly specific…"*: Aaron T. Beck, A. John Rush, Brian F. Shaw, and Gary Emery, *Cognitive Therapy of Depression* (New York: Guilford Press, 1987), 4.

203   *"The behavioral aspect of CBT…"*: Rashmi Nemade, Natalie Staats Reiss, and Mark Dombeck, "Cognitive Behavioral Therapy for Major Depression Continued," MentalHelp .net. Available at http://www.mentalhelp.net/poc/view_doc .php?type=doc&id=13025&cn=5.

203 "*[With] cognitive rehearsal the patient…*": Paula Ford-Martin, "Behavioral Therapy," Healthline.com. Available at http://www.healthline.com/galecontent/behavioral-therapy/2.

204 "*Cognitive-behavioral therapy has been shown…*": Charles Barber, *Comfortably Numb: How Psychiatry Is Medicating a Nation* (New York: Vintage Books, 2008), 152.

208 "*A necessary condition for widespread depressive illness…*": David A. Karp, *Speaking of Sadness: Depression, Disconnection, and the Meanings of Illness* (New York: Oxford University Press, 1996), 172–73.

210 "*Sadness is an inherent part of the human condition…*": Allan Horwitz and Jerome Wakefield, *The Loss of Sadness: How Psychiatry Transformed Normal Sorrow into Depressive Disorder* (New York: Oxford University Press, 2007), 225.

BIBLIOGRAPHY

Anderson, Walter Truitt, ed. *The Truth about the Truth: De-confusing and Re-constructing the Postmodern World.* New York: Jeremy Tarcher, 1995.

Arendt, Hannah. *The Human Condition.* Chicago: University of Chicago Press, 1958.

Baggini, Julian. *What's It All About: Philosophy and the Meaning of Life.* New York: Oxford University Press, 2004.

Barber, Charles. *Comfortably Numb: How Psychiatry Is Medicating a Nation.* New York: Vintage Books, 2008.

Barnes, Hazel E. *An Existentialist Ethics.* New York: Knopf, 1967.

Barrett, William. *Irrational Man: A Study in Existential Philosophy,* New York: Doubleday, 1962.

Baumel, Syd. *Dealing with Depression Naturally.* New York: McGraw-Hill, 2000.

Beauvoir, Simone de. *The Second Sex.* Trans. H. M. Parshley. New York: Vintage Books, 1949.

Beck, Aaron, A. John Rush, Brian Shaw, and Gary Emery. *Cognitive Therapy of Depression.* New York: Guilford Press, 1987.

Becker, Ernest. *The Birth and Death of Meaning.* New York: The Free Press, 1971.

Bentall, Richard. *Doctoring the Mind: Is Our Current Treatment of Mental Illness Really Any Good?* New York: New York University Press, 2009.

Blackham, H. J. *Six Existential Thinkers*. New York: Harper and Row, 1959.

Breggin, Peter. *Medication Madness*. New York: St. Martin's Press, 2009.

———. *Talking Back to Prozac*. New York: St. Martin's Press, 1995.

Busch, Tomas. *Circulating Being: From Embodiment to Incorporation (Essays on Late Existentialism)*. New York: Fordham University Press, 1999.

Butler, Judith. *Gender Trouble: Feminism and the Subversion of Identity*. New York: Routledge, 1990.

Carlat, Daniel. *Unhinged: The Trouble with Psychiatry — A Doctor's Revelations about a Profession in Crisis*. New York: Free Press, 2010.

Carr, David. *Time, Narrative, and History*. Bloomington: Indiana University Press, 1986.

Carroll, John, ed. *Language, Thought and Reality: Selected Writings of Benjamin Lee Whorf*. New York: Wiley, 1956.

Camus, Albert. *Exile and the Kingdom*. Trans. Justin O'Brien. New York: Vintage Books, 1957.

———. *The Fall*. Trans. Justin O'Brien. New York: Knopf, 1956.

———. *The Myth of Sisyphus and Other Essays*. Trans. Justin O'Brien. New York: Knopf, 1955.

———. *The Plague*. Trans. Stuart Gilbert. New York: Random House, 1946.

———. *The Rebel*. Trans. Anthony Bower. New York: Knopf, 1956.

———. *Resistance, Rebellion and Death*. Trans. Justin O'Brien. New York: Knopf, 1960.

———. *The Stranger*. Trans. Matthew Ward. New York: Knopf, 1988.

Collins, James. *The Existentialists: A Critical Study*. Chicago: Henry Regnery Company, 1952.

———. *Uncommon Cultures*. New York: Routledge, 1989.

Conrad, Peter. *The Medicalization of Society: On the Transformation of Human Conditions into Treatable Disorders*. Baltimore: Johns Hopkins Press, 2007.

Cooper, D. *Existentialism*. Oxford: Blackwell, 1999.

Dienstag, Joshua. *Pessimism: Philosophy, Ethic, Spirit*. Princeton, NJ: Princeton University Press, 2009.

Dobzhansky, Theodosius. *The Biological Basis of Human Freedom*. New York: Columbia University Press, 1956.

Dostoevsky, Fyodor. *The Brothers Karamazov*. Trans. Constance Garnett. Translation revised by Ralph E. Matlaw. New York: Norton, 1976.

Earnshaw, Steven. *Existentialism: A Guide for the Perplexed*. London: Continuum, 2006.

Emmons, Henry, and Rachel Kranz. *The Chemistry of Joy: A Three-Step Program for Overcoming Depression through Western Science and Eastern Wisdom*. New York: Fireside Books, 2005.

Fabry, Joseph. *The Pursuit of Meaning: Viktor Frankl, Logotherapy, and Life*. New York: Harper and Row, 1968.

Fadiman, James, and Don Kewman, eds. *Exploring Madness: Experience, Theory, and Research*. Monterey, CA: Brooks/Cole Publishing, 1973.

Flanagan, Owen. *The Really Hard Problem: Meaning in a Material World*. Cambridge, MA: MIT Press, 2007.

Flynn, Thomas. *Existentialism: A Very Short Introduction*. New York: Oxford University Press, 2006.

Foucault, Michel. *The Archaeology of Knowledge & the Discourse on Language*. New York: Pantheon, 1972.

Frankl, Viktor. *Man's Search for Meaning: An Introduction to Logotherapy*. New York: Pocket Books, 1959.

———. *Psychotherapy and Existentialism: Selected Papers on Logotherapy*. New York: Simon & Schuster, 1967.

———. *The Unheard Cry for Meaning: Psychotherapy and Humanism*. New York: Simon & Schuster, 1978.

Friedman, Maurice, ed. *The Worlds of Existentialism: A Critical Reader*. Chicago: University of Chicago Press, 1964.

Gardner, Howard. *Multiple Intelligences: New Horizons in Theory and Practice*. New York: Basic Books, 2006.

Gelven, Michael. *The Risk of Being: What It Means to Be Good and Bad*. University Park: Penn State Press, 1997.

———. *Truth and Existence: A Philosophical Inquiry*. University Park: Penn State Press, 1990.

Gergen, Kenneth. *The Saturated Self: Dilemmas of Identity in Contemporary Life*. New York: Basic Books, 1991.

Goleman, Daniel. *Emotional Intelligence: Why It Can Matter More Than IQ*. 10th anniversary edition. New York: Bantam, 2006.

Gordon, Haim, ed. *Dictionary of Existentialism*. New York: Greenwood Press, 1999.

Gordon, James. *Unstuck: Your Guide to the Seven-Stage Journey out of Depression*. New York: Penguin, 2009.

Gordon, Lewis, ed. *Existence in Black: An Anthology of Black Existential Philosophy*. New York: Routledge, 1997.

———. *Existentia Africana: Understanding Africana Existential Thought*. London: Routledge, 2000.

Greenberg, Gary. *Manufacturing Depression: The Secret History of a Modern Disease*. New York: Simon & Schuster, 2010.

Grene, Majorie Glicksman. *Dreadful Freedom: A Critique of Existentialism*. Chicago: University of Chicago Press, 1948.

Guignon, Charles, et al., ed. *The Existentialists: Critical Essays on Kierkegaard, Nietzsche, Heidegger, and Sartre*. New York: Rowman and Littlefield, 2003.

Guillebeau, Chris. *The Art of Non-conformity: Set Your Own Rules, Live the Life You Want, and Change the World*. New York: Perigee Trade Books, 2010.

Habermas, Jürgen. *Legitimation Crisis*. Trans. Thomas McCarthy. Boston: Beacon Press, 1975.

Harvey, David. *The Condition of Postmodernity: An Enquiry into the Origins of Cultural Change*. Cambridge: Basil Blackwell, 1989.

Heidegger, Martin. *Being and Time*. Trans. John Macquarrie and Edward Robinson. New York: Harper and Row, 1962.

Hook, Sidney, ed. *Determinism and Freedom in the Age of Modern Science*. New York: Collier Books, 1958.

Horwitz, Allan. *Creating Mental Illness*. Chicago: University of Chicago Press, 2003.

Horwitz, Allan, and Jerome Wakefield. *The Loss of Sadness: How Psychiatry Transformed Normal Sorrow into Depression Disorder*. New York: Oxford University Press, 2007.

Ilardi, Stephen. *The Depression Cure: The 6-Step Program to Beat Depression without Drugs*. New York: Da Capo Lifelong Books, 2010.

Ionesco, Eugene. *Fragments of a Journal.* Trans. Jean Stewart. New York: Grove Press, 1968.

Jaspers, Karl. *Reason and Existenz: Five Lectures.* New York: Noonday Press, 1968.

Judt, Tony. *Past Imperfect: French Intellectuals 1944–1956.* Berkeley and Los Angeles: University of California Press, 1992.

Kafka, Franz. *The Castle.* Trans. Willa and Edwin Muir. New York: Penguin Books, 1930.

———. *The Metamorphosis.* Trans. Stanley Corngold. New York: Schocken Books, 1972.

———. *The Trial.* New York: Knopf, 1937.

Karl, Frederick, and Leo Hamalian, eds. *The Existential Imagination.* New York: Premier Books, 1963.

Karp, David. *Speaking of Sadness: Depression, Disconnection, and the Meanings of Illness.* New York: Oxford University Press, 1996.

Kaufmann, Walter, ed. *Existentialism from Dostoevsky to Sartre.* Cleveland: Meridian Books, 1968.

Kierkegaard, Søren. *Concluding Unscientific Postscript.* Trans. David F. Swenson and Walter Lowrie. Princeton, NJ: Princeton University Press, 1971.

———. *Fear and Trembling.* Trans. Howard V. Hong and Edna H. Hong. Princeton, NJ: Princeton University Press, 1983.

Kirsch, Irvin. *The Emperor's New Drugs: Exploding the Antidepressant Myth.* New York: Basic Books, 2010.

Korsgaard, Christine. *The Sources of Normativity.* Cambridge: Cambridge University Press, 1996.

Kruks, Sonia. *Situation and Human Existence: Freedom, Subjectivity, and Society.* London: Unwin Hyman, 1990.

Leventhal, Allan, and Christophe Martell. *The Myth of Depression as Disease: Limitations and Alternatives to Drug Treatment.* New York: Praeger, 2005.

Lyotard, Jean-François. *The Postmodern Condition.* Minneapolis: University of Minnesota Press, 1984.

Maisel, Eric. *The Atheist's Way: Living Well Without Gods.* Novato, CA: New World Library, 2009.

———. *Coaching the Artist Within: Advice for Writers, Actors, Visual*

Artists, and Musicians from America's Foremost Creativity Coach.
Novato, CA: New World Library, 2005.

———. *Ten Zen Seconds: Twelve Incantations for Purpose, Power, and Calm.* Naperville, IL: Sourcebooks, 2007.

———. *The Van Gogh Blues: The Creative Person's Path through Depression.* Novato, CA: New World Library, 2002.

Marcel, Gabriel. *Being and Having.* Trans. Katherine Farrer. London: Westminster, 1949.

———. *The Philosophy of Existentialism,* New York: Citadel Press, 1968.

May, Rollo. *The Discovery of Being: Writings in Existential Psychology.* New York: Norton, 1994.

———, ed. *Existential Psychology.* New York: Random House, 1969.

———. *Man's Search for Himself.* New York: Dell, 1953.

McBride, William, ed. *The Development and Meaning of Twentieth Century Existentialism.* New York: Garland Publishers, 1997.

McKay, Martha, Matthew Davis, and Patrick Fanning. *Thoughts and Feelings: Taking Control of Your Moods and Your Life.* Oakland, CA: New Harbinger Publications, 2007.

Merleau-Ponty, Maurice. *Adventures of the Dialectic.* Trans. Joseph Bien. Evanston: Northwestern University Press, 1973.

———. *The Phenomenology of Perception.* Trans. Colin Smith. New York: Routledge and Kegan Paul, 1962.

Moncrieff, Joanna. *The Myth of the Chemical Cure: A Critique of Psychiatric Drug Treatment.* New York: Palgrave MacMillan, 2009.

Moran, Richard. *Authority and Estrangement: An Essay on Self Knowledge.* Princeton, NJ: Princeton University Press, 2001.

Nehamas, Alexander. *The Art of Living: Socratic Reflections from Plato to Foucault.* Berkeley and Los Angeles: University of California Press, 1998.

Nietzsche, Friedrich. *The Gay Science.* Trans. Walter Kaufmann. New York: Vintage Books, 1974.

———. *On the Genealogy of Morals.* Trans. Walter Kaufmann. New York: Vintage Books, 1969.

———. *Thus Spoke Zarathustra: A Book for All and None.* In *The*

Portable Nietzsche. Trans. Walter Kaufmann. New York: Viking Press, 1975.

Nisbet, Robert. *History of the Idea of Progress.* New York: Basic Books, 1980.

O'Connor, Richard. *Undoing Depression.* New York: Little, Brown and Company, 2010.

Olafson, Frederick. *Principles and Persons: An Ethical Interpretation of Existentialism.* Baltimore: Johns Hopkins Press, 1967.

Ortega y Gasset, José. *The Revolt of the Masses.* Trans. Anthony Kerrigan. Notre Dame: University of Notre Dame Press, 1985.

Reynolds, Jack. *Understanding Existentialism.* London: Acumen, 2006.

Ricoeur, Paul. *Oneself as Another.* Trans. Kathleen Blamey. Chicago: University of Chicago Press, 1992.

Samuels, Andrew. *The Plural Psyche: Personality, Morality, and the Father.* London: Routledge, 1993.

Sartre, Jean-Paul. *Being and Nothingness.* Trans. Hazel Barnes. New York: Washington Square Press, 1992.

———. *Existentialism Is a Humanism.* Trans. Carol Macomber. New Haven: Yale University Press, 2007.

———. *Nausea.* Trans. Lloyd Alexander. New York: New Directions, 1959.

———. *No Exit, and Three Other Plays.* New York: Vintage Books, 1955.

Schneider, Kirk, and Orah Krug. *Existential-Humanistic Therapy.* New York: American Psychological Association Press, 2009.

Shorter, Edward. *Before Prozac: The Troubled History of Mood Disorders in Psychiatry.* New York: Oxford University Press, 2008.

Solomon, Robert, ed. *Existentialism.* New York: Random House, 1974.

Spiegelberg, E. *The Phenomenological Movement: A Historical Introduction,.* 3rd ed. The Hague: Martinus Nijhoff, 1984.

Szasz, Thomas. *The Manufacture of Madness: A Comparative Study of the Inquisition and the Mental Health Movement.* Syracuse, NY: Syracuse University Press, 1997.

———. *The Medicalization of Everyday Life: Selected Essays.* Syracuse, NY: Syracuse University Press, 2007.

———. *The Myth of Mental Illness: Foundations of a Theory of Personal Conduct.* New York: Harper Perennial, 2010.

————. *The Myth of Psychotherapy: Mental Healing as Religion, Rhetoric and Repression.* Syracuse, NY: Syracuse University Press, 1988.

Taylor, Charles. *Sources of the Self: The Making of the Modern Identity.* Cambridge MA: Harvard University Press, 1989.

Tillich, Paul. *The Courage to Be.* New Haven: Yale University Press, 2000.

Unamuno, Miguel de. *The Tragic Sense of Life.* Trans. J. E. Crawford Flitch. New York: Dover, 1954.

Van Deurzen, Emmy. *Everyday Mysteries: A Handbook of Existential Psychotherapy.* New York: Routledge, 2010.

————. *Existential Counseling and Psychotherapy in Practice.* London: Sage Publications, 2002.

Vincent, Norah. *Voluntary Madness: Lost and Found in the Mental Healthcare System.* New York: Penguin, 2009.

Wahl, Jean. *A Short History of Existentialism.* Trans. Forrest Williams and Stanley Maron. New York: Philosophical Library, 1949.

Warnock, Mary. *Existentialist Ethics.* London: Macmillan, 1967.

Watters, Ethan. *Crazy Like Us: The Globalization of the American Psyche.* New York: Free Press, 2010.

Whitaker, Robert. *Anatomy of an Epidemic: Magic Bullets, Psychiatric Drugs, and the Astonishing Rise of Mental Illness in America.* New York: Crown, 2010.

————. *Mad in America: Bad Science, Bad Medicine, and the Enduring Mistreatment of the Mentally Ill.* New York: Basic Books.

Wild, John Daniel. *The Challenge of Existentialism.* Bloomington: Indiana University Press, 1963.

Williams, Mark, John Teasdale, Zindel Segal, and Jon Kabat-Zinn. *The Mindful Way through Depression: Freeing Yourself from Chronic Unhappiness.* New York: The Guilford Press, 2007.

Wilson, Colin. *The Outsider.* New York: Dell, 1956.

Yalom, Irvin. *Existential Psychotherapy.* New York: Basic Books, 1980.

Zaner, Richard, and Don Ihde, eds. *Phenomenology and Existentialism.* New York: Capricorn Books, 1973.

INDEX

doubt, 83–84, 154
drugs, 20, 22, 30, 41
"dysmoveria," as mental disorder,
    17–20

E

emotional intelligence, 117
Emperor's New Drugs, The
    (Kirsch), 35
engagement, 86, 146, 153
ethics, 97
euphoria, 124
excellence, 170–71
existence
    acceptance of, 78–79
    facts of, 135–40, 146
    See also life
existential anxiety, 55, 146, 177–78
Existential Counseling and
    Psychotherapy in Practice (van
    Deurzen), 187–88
existential depression, 208
existential dread, 55
existential freedom, 83, 87
Existential Imagination, The (Karl
    and Hamalian), 190–91
existential intelligence
    average vs. high, 119–21
    defined, 118
    measurement of, 118
    obstacles to using, 123
    origin of term, 115–18
    as primary intelligence,
        118–19
    using, 59

existentialism
    central message of, 1, 53,
        78–79
    ideals of, 52–56, 135
    post-WWII popularity of, 78
    pre-Socratic Greek, 126
    trademarks of, 55
    unpopularity of, 53–55
existential plan
    advantages of following,
        210–12
    elements of, 57–62
    goal of, 56–57
    tactics used for, 151, 156
    See also meaning; meaning
        investments; meaning-
        making; *specific aspect*
existential self-care, 61, 184,
    187–92
experimentation, 172

F

Fanning, Patrick, 195
fatigue, 178–81
fear and trembling, 55
Fischer, Bobby, 121
freedom, 146
Freud, Sigmund, 51–52
Friedman, Maurice, 56

G

Gardner, Howard, 116–18, 119
German Institute for Quality and
    Efficiency in Health Care, 32
Goleman, Daniel, 117

J

jobs
- meaning crises at, 178–85
- meaning investment at, 164–65
- as meaning opportunity, 173
- performance at, 12–13
- satisfaction at, 50

Journal of Consulting and Clinical Psychology, 29

Journal of Nervous and Mental Disease, 27–28

Journal of the American Medical Association, 32–33

K

Kafka, Franz, 53
Karl, Frederick, 190–91
Karp, David, 208–9
Kelley, John, 33

L

Langer, Ellen, 28–29
language, replacing, 157
leisure time, managing, 165
life
- appreciating, 174–75
- authentic, 56–57, 76, 78, 80–81
- dealing with facts of, 59, 135–40, 190
- death contrasted with, 78
- looking in the eye, 57, 63–67, 154
- as project, 209–10
- questions for orientation to, 204–5
- unhappiness with, 51
- as unique, 65, 76–77

life-purpose vision, 58
- central function of, as existential chime, 111
- creating, 105–10
- employing, 110–13
- examples, 106–7
- existential intelligence and, 115
- revising, 112
- wants/needs/values coordinated in, 104

linguistic intelligence, 117
logical-mathematical intelligence, 117

Loss of Sadness, The (Horwitz and Wakefield), 210

lottery winners, unhappiness of, 207–8

love, 169–70
lovelessness, 50, 66–67

M

Mad in America (Whitaker), 29–30

Manufacture of Madness, The (Szasz), 36

Matisse, Henri, 54
mattering
- decision on the process of, 58, 89–96

trance
cultural, 129–30, 131–32
personal, 129
snapping out of, 59, 130–31
treatments, 19–20
antidepressants, 31–35
diagnosis and, 30–31
profit motive in, 37–38
psychotherapy, 35–38
use of term, by mental health
industry, 41–42
See also antidepressants;
psychotherapy

U

unhappiness
accepting reality of, 52, 136,
137
anger mixed with, 178–81
anxiety mixed with, 178–81
authentic life and, 211
"depression" as, 2, 11, 39–40
depression as different from,
41
existential plan to eliminate,
56–57
fatigue mixed with, 178–81
of lottery winners, 207–8
meaning crises as cause of,
177
as mental disorder, 3, 10–12,
49
mood and, 124–25, 128

as normal human experience,
208, 209–10
reasons for, 49–51, 66–67, 83
"symptoms" of, 10
thoughts as cause of, 195
universality of, 49, 51–52
universe, meaninglessness of, 80,
83, 86
unwanted life aspects
as abnormal, 9–10, 12
as mental disorder, 20–21
as psychological disorder, 35

V

values
appetite vs., 97–98
contextualizing, 98
contradictory, 98, 101
conundrums in choosing,
101–2
experimenting with, 102–4
honoring, 58
list of, 98–101
van Deurzen, Emmy, 187–88
visualization, 160–61
vitalism, 76–77
vocabulary of meaning, 60
basic phrases, 141–42
building, 144–50
during morning meaning
practice, 157
need for, 141
as tactic, 151, 156
using, 143–44
void, the, 125–27, 191

ABOUT THE AUTHOR

ERIC MAISEL, PHD, the author of forty books, is widely regarded as America's foremost creativity coach. He trains creativity coaches nationally and internationally and provides core trainings for the Creativity Coaching Association. He writes a regular column for *Professional Artist* magazine and the "Rethinking Depression" blog for *Psychology Today*. In addition, he is crafting a new philosophy of meaning called noimetics. His books include *Coaching the Artist Within*, *Creative Recovery*, *Fearless Creating*, *The Van Gogh Blues*, and many others. Three of his classes are available through the Academy for Optimal Living: Your Best Life in the Arts, Infinite Meaning, and the companion class to this book, Rethinking Depression. Maisel lives in the San Francisco Bay Area with his family.

His website is www.ericmaisel.com.

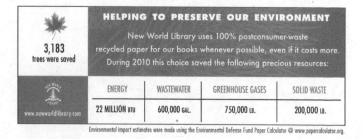